W9-APG-250

THOMAS MERTON
IN SEARCH OF
HIS SOUL

271.12
WAL

THOMAS MERTON IN SEARCH OF HIS SOUL

• A JUNGIAN PERSPECTIVE •

ROBERT G. WALDRON

AVE MARIA PRESS Notre Dame, Indiana 46556

Excerpts are taken from the NEW REVISED STANDARD VERSION, copyright © 1991 by Oxford University Press, Inc. Reprinted by permission of the publisher.

"All the Way Down" and "Hagia Sophia" are reprinted from *Collected Poems of Thomas Merton*, copyright © 1963 by The Abbey of Gethsemani, Inc., 1977 by the Trustees of the Merton Legacy Trust. Reprinted by permission of New Directions Publishing Corp.

Excerpts from *A Vow of Conversation* by Thomas Merton, copyright © 1988 by the Merton Legacy Trust. Reprinted by permission of Farrar, Straus, Giroux, Inc.

Excerpts from *The Seven Storey Mountain* by Thomas Merton, copyright © 1948 by Harcourt Brace & Co. Reprinted by permission.

Excerpts from *Carl G. Jung, Psychological Reflections*, copyright © 1973 by Princeton University Press. Reprinted by permission of Princeton University Press.

© 1994 by Ave Maria Press, Notre Dame, IN 46556

All rights reserved. No part of this book may be used or reproduced in any manner whatsoever without written permission, except in the case of reprints in the context of reviews.

International Standard Book Number: 0-87793-524-6

Library of Congress Catalog Card Number: 93-74198

Book design and illustration by Elizabeth J. French

Printed and bound in the United States of America.

LIBRARY
SAINT MARY'S CONVENT
NOTRE DAME, INDIANA

Dedicated to the memory of my brother,
Kevin T. Waldron

ACKNOWLEDGMENTS

I extend heartfelt thanks to all my mentors who either encouraged me during the writing of this book or read and edited portions of it:

Patrick Brown, monk of St. Joseph's Abbey, Spencer, Massachusettes; Jonathan Montaldo, Robert Daggy, Juanita Ponte, Francis Cahill, Robert Cox, Robert Tarpey, Thomas Kloss, Maryann Muhilly, James Doherty, Margaret Waldron, Robert Flynn, Mary MacLean, Joseph Neary, Julia Renna, Kevin Roche, and Lillian McCourt.

Special thanks to Rev. Robert Baer who taught me everything I know about Carl Jung and to The National Endowment for the Humanities, *The Merton Seasonal*, *The Merton Annual* and my editor, Robert Hamma.

CONTENTS

PREFACE

This book is the culmination of several years of reading, study, and reflection. I would like to think that Merton—writer *par excellence* of silence, solitude, and reflection—would approve of the final product. My purpose in writing this book is to illustrate how the course of Merton's life is not merely similar to Jung's paradigm of individuation, but identical to it. Consequently, Jung's analytic psychology provides illuminative insights concerning what Merton called his "interior journey."

This book is not offered as a biography of Thomas Merton. Several fine biographies have already been published, including the definitive one written by Michael Mott. Other biographies written by Merton's fellow monks and friends offer intimate glimpses into Merton's life as a monk, priest, writer, poet, and social critic. I think of those by Brother Patrick Hart, Monica Furlong, Basil Pennington, and William Shannon.

Thomas Merton: A Jungian Commentary is, as the title indicates, a commentary. Therefore, its format is brief and highly focused. From his autobiographical writing, both prose and poetry, I examine essential stages in Merton's life which propelled him on his inner journey to wholeness. During these stages Merton gained insights of self-knowledge, although he was not always fully conscious of the significance of these stages at the time they occurred. Full awareness sometimes took years to be achieved. Often it was through his dreams that Merton learned life-enhancing truths about himself. Thus, I devote two chapters to a close analysis of several of Merton's pivotal dreams, interpreting them from a Jungian perspective.

It is my intent that this commentary will assist readers in achieving a deeper understanding of Merton's life, of what he faced and overcame during his journey. It is my hope that we may more readily appreciate the *universal nature* of his journey. His life is, I believe, an inspiration to each one of us who is seeking to live a life which is more fully human, whole, and more Christlike.

Although I do not see the development of personality as linear (it is in my opinion more like a spiral), I analyze Merton's life chronologically, beginning with his adolescence, continuing through his early adulthood, onto his years as a young monk, and concluding with his maturity. I rely heavily on certain volumes and poems: *The Seven Storey Mountain* (his autobiography), *Seeds of Contemplation, The Sign of Jonas*, poems such as "Hagia Sophia," "All the Way Down," and the posthumously published journal, *A Vow of Conversation*.

I have been reading and studying Merton for twenty years, Jung for eleven. I came to see that Jung profoundly understood the kind of spiritual malaise Merton endured and overcame. Jung's work with his patients led him to the belief that modern men and women had lost touch with their souls, resulting in a psychic condition that invariably found life to be meaningless. Thus it became Jung's *raison d'etre* to assist people in rediscovering their souls, aiding them in their search for meaning, all culminating in his psychological theory of **individuation**.

The benefit of employing Jung's analytic psychology as a tool toward understanding Merton's search for meaning is that with such an aid we not only achieve a deeper appreciation of Thomas Merton's life and work, but we also achieve a deeper understanding of our own inner journey. For according to Jung every journey is the same in that it has one goal: the archetypal **Self**. I must acknowledge here that Anne E. Carr's observation concerning the connection between Jung and Merton encouraged me to proceed with my Jungian analysis of Merton's life and work. After noting how Merton's search for self corresponded in some ways to Freudian theory, she writes:

> Perhaps even stronger is the correspondence with Jungian theory suggested by the pattern of individuation from the ego to the self, through conscious acceptance of the dark self or shadow (for a man, the anima, his feminine side) and the importance of the persona and religious myth in this process. One could argue that Merton's highly individuated self, both as an untypical monk and as a creative writer, exemplify Jung's psychological pattern very aptly.[1]

In writing this book about Merton's "pattern of individuation," I have assumed that readers will have some knowledge of both Merton and Jung. For those new to Jung, I have included a glossary of the most commonly used Jungian terms as well as other psychological terms. (These terms appear in bold the first time they are used in the text.)

INTRODUCTION

The widespread popularity of Thomas Merton's autobiography *The Seven Storey Mountain* is one of the most unexpected literary events of our time. Since its publication in 1948, it has never been out of print, and it has been translated into seventeen languages. Why would the story of a young man entering the Trappists, one of the strictest contemplative orders of the Catholic church, be a bestseller? Thomas Merton's autobiography became a symbol for his generation, possibly for this century; he was Carl Jung's "modern man in search of a soul." To many disillusioned, bewildered, postwar readers shaken by the horrors of World War II and frightened by the uncertainties of the atomic age, a brilliant young man's sacrifice of everything for God appeared heroic if not incredible. Merton's autobiography resonated with their own confusion, desires, fears, and preoccupations. They were heartened to discover that within their own cultural traditions they could still find spiritual and psychic nourishment. This was Merton's testament to Western readers: Christianity in the twentieth century is still very much alive, it offers to everyone a meaningful way of life based upon the life and teaching of Jesus Christ.

Merton realized that what was true for him was universal. Like Emerson he understood the transcendental wisdom, "To believe your own thought, to believe that what is true for you in your private heart, is true for all men: that is genius."[1] In one of his most popular books, *New Seeds of Contemplation*, Merton reiterates this Emersonian insight when he writes "We are one man." His readers embraced this innate wisdom: the original clothbound edition of *The Seven Storey Mountain* sold 600,000 copies!

Another inspiring twentieth century autobiography is Carl Jung's *Memories, Dreams, Reflections* (1961) which chronicles Jung's search for meaning and wholeness in his life. Whereas Merton sought meaning and wholeness via an ancient tradition, Catholic monasticism, Jung sought meaning and wholeness via humanity's newest science, psychology. The goal of both men's search is similar, if not the same: Jung's goal is the archetype of wholeness he calls the Self; Merton's goal is Christ. And for Jung the Self is Christ.

Unlike Freud who considered religion a form of neurosis, Carl Jung deeply understood the intrinsic value of religion. He was raised in a Christian family; his father was a minister as were seven of his uncles. He fully appreciated the religious impulse in himself and in all people. In 1952 he wrote to a young clergyman, "I find that all my thoughts circle around God like the planets around the sun, and are as irresistibly attracted by Him. I would feel it to be the grossest sin if I were to oppose any resistance to this force."[2] Thus Jung's analytic psychology incorporates religion. It theorizes that modern people suffering neurosis have "lost what the living religions of every age have given to their followers and none of them has been really healed who did not regain this religious outlook."[3]

Thomas Merton saved himself from a life of decadence, if not suicide, by developing a religious outlook on life. In my discussion of Merton, I shall illustrate how his spiritual journey, which he recorded in numerous autobiographical works, in prose and poetry, exemplifies the archetypal journey toward wholeness, understood more fully in the light of Carl Jung's analytic psychology, specifically his theory of individuation.

What is individuation? According to Jungian Aniela Jaffe, the individuation process involves developing/exploring the divine spark within each of us. When asked what the religious function of humanity is, she said: "His individuation. Nothing else. This is his religious function, to show God what He/She has put in me, with good and with bad, the shadow in life, both."[4]

Jung states that the ultimate goal of individuation is to discover the archetypal Self. He writes:

> The Self is a circle whose center is everywhere and whose circumference is nowhere.... And do you know where the Self is for Western man? It is Christ, for Christ is the archetype of the hero, representing man's highest aspiration. All this is very mysterious and at times frightening.[5]

According to Jung, when an individual is in touch with the Christ within, he becomes "himself, whole, indivisible and distinct from other people though also in relations to these."[6] Jung's use of the word whole in his description of an individuated person suggests not a pristine form of perfection, but a mature kind of completeness. In his youth Jung was very much puzzled by Christ's injunction to all people to be perfect, "Be perfect, therefore, as your heavenly Father is perfect" (Mt 5:48), for he believed no person could ever during life achieve perfection. He observed that the Greek root *teleios*, most often translated as perfect, is closer in meaning to whole or complete. He preferred the latter translation because he believed the pursuit of perfection would end only in frustration and failure. To Jung perfection is a universe of a difference away from wholeness or completeness. In writing to a Benedictine priest, he explains:

> You yourself feel the need for a definition of "perfection." You define it as the "complete unfolding of nature on the level of holiness, brought about by surrendering to God." In so far as God is wholeness himself, himself whole and holy, man attains his wholeness only in God, that is, in self-completeness, which in turn he attains only by submitting to God's will. Since man in the state of wholeness and holiness is far from any kind of "perfection," the New Testament *teleios* must surely be translated as "complete." For me the state of human wholeness is one of "completeness" and not of "perfection," an expression, like "holiness," I tend to avoid.[7]

From the beginning of his conversion, Merton, however, took Christ's command to be perfect quite literally. This created frustration for him, compounded by his taking to heart his friend Robert Lax's suggestion that the only worthwhile ambition in life was sainthood, a dangerous ambition because it was prideful. Merton's journey, then, created for itself unrealistic hurdles resulting in wasted years and energy before he realized what was important in the pursuit of wholeness. In the end, he settled for being ordinary and fully human, or to put it more simply, he learned to be himself. Indeed, the very intensity of Merton's autobiography, which rivets readers, derives from the discordance between what Merton thinks he should be (a saint) and what he is (a fallible person).

Prior to his conversion Merton nurtured his growing spirituality on two books recommended to him by his Hindu friend Bramachari: Augustine's *Confessions* and Thomas á Kempis' *The Imitation of Christ*. Such spiritual commentaries recommend a pursuit of holiness which fosters the notion that the less human one is the more holy one is. Thomas á Kempis exhorts the Christian: "Truly to know and despise oneself is the best and most perfect council." Not wise advice for one such as Merton who as a young man saw himself as a great sinner. This self-image led Merton to a self-loathing which in turn he **projected** onto the world, resulting in what is commonly known as Merton's early *contemptus mundi*.

Jung was very much aware of the kind of spiritual snare to which Merton was subjected, one that ignores human fallibility, human weakness. He wisely warns all those who embark on the inner journey not to lose sight of their humanity:

> To strive for perfection is a high ideal. But I say fulfill something you are able to fulfill rather than run after what you will never achieve. Nobody is perfect. Remember the saying: "No one is good but God alone" (Lk 18:19). And nobody can be. We can modestly strive to fulfill ourselves and to be as complete human beings as possible, and that will be trouble enough.[8]

When Merton converted to Catholicism, he was mesmerized by the stereotype of saintliness promoted by such books as *The Imitation of Christ*. His early biography of a Trappistine abbess, Mother Berchmans, entitled *Exile Ends in Glory* (a book Merton later rated as "bad") is fraught with cruel, inhuman descriptions of austerity, obviously accepted if not advocated by the author, an enthusiastic convert whose ideas of holiness were rigid and unhealthy. Such ideas and practices are understandable when we consider that Merton faced tremendous problems involving his personal sense of guilt. He had yet to come to terms with his **shadow**, the unconscious portion of the personality usually characterized by negative traits or attitudes which the conscious **ego** rejects or ignores. Consequently, he felt a need for an asceticism which was harsh and demanding, one that would purge himself of his sins. He describes himself as a novice:

> During the first period, after entering the monastery, I was totally isolated from all outside influences and was largely working with what I had accumulated before entering. [I drew] on the experience of the monastic life in my early years when I was quite ascetic, "first fervor" stuff, and when the life at Gethsemani was very strict. This resulted in an highly unworldly, ascetical, intransigent, somewhat apocalyptic outlook. Rigid, arbitrary separation between God and the world.[9]

Merton would outgrow this life-denying spirituality, exhibiting little compassion toward himself or the world, but only after encountering his own shadow and **anima**, finally culminating in a religious breakthrough in 1958, an experience often referred to as the Louisville Vision. This experience would lead him toward an understanding that holiness does not demand renunciation of the world. True sanctity, he would learn, encourages self-acceptance which in turn compassionately embraces the world.

During the early years in his religious life, however, Merton opted for a spiritual discipline nourished by the writing of the ascetic desert fathers and the austere St. John of the Cross, who for many years was Merton's favorite mystic and whose mystical theology Merton addressed in his full-length study *The Ascent of Truth*. Later in his life his spiritual mentors would be the fourteenth century mystic Lady Julian of Norwich and the modern mystic Raissa Maritain, the wife of Merton's good friend Jacques Maritain. Their spirituality was founded on love and compassion rather than on an anti-human asceticism, characteristic of St. John of the Cross and the Trappist order itself.

Merton's self-negation and world denial very likely originated during his earliest years with his mother—whose standards of behavior for her son were nothing short of perfection itself, who denied her son a last embrace as she died of cancer in a hospital. Was his choice of the severe Trappist order a substitute for the severe mother he lost when he was six years old? Were the Trappist standards of behavior just as unrealistic? Was Merton's first, negative experience of the feminine to haunt him for the rest of his life? These are some of the questions to be addressed in the following chapters. But the important thing to keep in mind is Merton's eventual willingness to face **consciously** his individuation. He learned that perfection, "an image without the slightest flaw," is a goal no human is capable of achieving. He comments on those who pursue it: they are "without humor as they are without wonder, without feeling and without interest in the common affairs of mankind."[10] He gradually realized that he, like all people, was a combination of spirit and flesh, man and woman, heaven and earth, child and adult, and light and dark. He realized all of this because his life depended upon it.

The following Jungian commentary on Thomas Merton's life will commence with the first hurdle of his individuation: his encounter with the shadow archetype. Addressing this aspect of individuation Jung calls the "apprentice-piece"[11] of a person's development. The closely associated psychological dynamics of ego/Self, persona/projection will also be addressed. The second part of this commentary will focus on Merton's encounter with his anima, the unconscious feminine side of his personality (a woman's unconscious masculine side is called her **animus**) whose recognition, acceptance, and integration into consciousness is necessary in order for a person to individuate. Jung describes this encounter with the anima (Latin "soul") as the "masterpiece"[12] of individuation.

There is little difference, if any, between the individuated person and the holy person. There are people who consider Merton to be a holy man, some a saint. Merton, however, certainly would have been loath to hear himself described as either. The traditional portrait of holiness as presented on "holy" cards with images of pining, fawning, or fainting saints embarrassed the mature Merton.[13] But he might have been more comfortable with being described as an individuated monk.

PART ONE

YOUNG MAN MERTON'S ENCOUNTER WITH HIS SHADOW

ONE

HIS FATHER'S DEATH: EMERGENCE OF THE SHADOW

> Everyone carries a shadow, and the less it is embodied in the individual's conscious life, the blacker and denser it is.[1]

Thomas Merton's unintegrated shadow looms throughout his autobiography *The Seven Storey Mountain*. When he was a young man, he felt its presence, resulting in a self-loathing which he projected onto the world. Merton's *contemptus mundi*, believing the world and himself in the world as evil, is a common psychological snare during the initial stages of the inner journey.

Jung identifies the shadow archetype as, "the thing a person has no wish to be."[2] It consists of all those aspects of ourselves that we would rather not face: our own evil. Too often we hide from our own evil (our sins) behind a *persona*. Derived from the Latin word meaning mask, the **persona** represented the masks actors wore in Greek and Roman theater to indicate the roles they were assuming. In life we all assume roles—at home, on the job, at social occasions—where we allow others to see only our good side, our best mask. The shadow, our negative side, remains hidden in the dark of the **unconscious**. It is often allowed expression only when there are no witnesses to it or when there are present others who share our shadow.

Once we accept the presence of our shadow in our psyche, we can learn to understand it by two methods: the first requires a conscious awareness of shadow projection; the second involves interpretation of dreams. Jung maintains that "projections change the world into the replica of one's own unknown face."[3] To know and understand our "unknown face," our shadow, we must develop an acute awareness of our opinions of other people, including our opinions of races, countries, and institutions. For example, when an individual is very critical of other people, bringing attention to faults he finds particularly annoying, it is quite likely that these grating faults are his own; and rather than face them, own them, he projects them onto others. Projection can be performed on an individual basis and also on a collective level. The Holocaust is an example of the collective projection by the German nation. Today's Japan bashing in America is also a kind of psychological projection.

When we accept and integrate our shadow, we liberate ourselves to see others as they really are as well as ourselves; thus, we grow in self-knowledge. The first important act, then, of individuation is for us to admit the reality of our shadow. Then we must befriend our shadow, allow its rightful presence in our consciousness. We must, like Shakespeare's Prospero, say, "This thing of darkness I acknowledge mine."[4]

Usually young people are unconcerned with their shadow. They are at a time of life when the ego sees itself as the center of the psyche. Young people in the morning of their lives are intent upon establishing themselves in the external world by vocation, marriage, and raising a family. Attending to spiritual needs, Jung says, is frequently relegated to the afternoon of life when the Self, the true center of the psyche, manifests itself in the form of a mid-life crisis, urging the individual to seek greater wholeness by embarking on the inner journey. A person at this time of crisis will usually undergo various kinds of anxiety, depression, low self-esteem, or a lassitude of spirit that finds life meaningless.

Thomas Merton's journey to wholeness does not exactly follow Jung's chronology of individuation. Merton was drawn into the inner journey during his middle adolescence, not at mid-life. Jungian Jolande Jacobi writes:

> Naturally there are also people who even in their youth seek more for the meaning of life, for inner spiritual values, than for the external, material, the earthly. They are the introverted, the seekers, the quiet, and reflective ones.... Many artists and scientists have derived from such an unusual fate, inspiration and strength for the creation of spiritually important work.[5]

Just eleven days short of his sixteenth birthday in 1931, Merton lost his father, Owen Merton, a talented artist, to a brain tumor. This death, in effect, ended Merton's childhood and catapulted him into the individuation process. From then on Merton's primary goal in life was somehow to discover the meaning of life and specifically the meaning of his own life.

LIBRARY
SAINT MARY'S CONVENT
NOTRE DAME, INDIANA

Merton writes movingly about his ill father. During his summer vacation Merton visited his father in the hospital,

> The sorrow of his great helplessness suddenly fell upon me like a mountain. I was crushed by it. The tears sprang to my eyes.... I hid my face in the blanket and cried. And poor father wept too.... There was nothing anyone could do.... What could I make of so much suffering? There was no way for me, or for anyone else in the family, to get anything out of it. It was a raw wound for which there was no adequate relief. You had to take it, like an animal.[6]

If we view this trauma as Merton's mid-life crisis, then Merton could say like Dante with whom he so much identified:

> When I had journeyed half of our life's way
> I found myself within a shadowed forest,
> For I had lost the path that does not stray.[7]

With his father's illness and imminent death, Merton finds himself lost in a forest of doubt, confusion, and guilt. Somehow he had to make sense of what appeared to be senseless; somehow he had to find answers to questions that appeared to be unanswerable. Unaware of it at the time, he already had embarked upon "the path that does not stray" which he later in life would describe as the "interior journey."

On one of his last visits to the hospital, he saw his father's bed covered by little sheets of blue paper with drawings similar to icons of Byzantine saints. This puzzled the young son because his father was not a particularly religious man, and his usual subjects for painting were natural scenes. Merton surmised that his father, within his tormented body, was somehow forging his own soul. Later this was a consolation to Merton who believed that his father may have saved his soul. And in a mysterious way these small scraps of paper foreshadowed Merton's own soul-making, signs of which we see not long after his father's death.

After his father's death, the young Merton remained depressed for two months and admits in his autobiography that he felt stripped of everything that would impede the movement of his own will. His ego was in complete control; he could now do as he pleased. He says the "the hard crust of my dry soul finally squeezed out all the last traces of religion that had ever been in it."[8] He saw himself as full of dust and rubbish, an Eliot hollow man.

From the vantage point of a thirty year old monk (1945), Merton describes his sixteen year old self:

> I now belonged to the world in which I lived. I became a true citizen of my disgusting century: the century of poison gas and atomic bombs ... a man with veins full of poison, living in death.[9]

Merton was filled guilt and hatred, hatred not only for himself but also for the world. Perhaps in some way he felt responsible for his father's death, that it was some malignity ("poison") inherent in him that destroyed his father. Perhaps he even felt guilty about the death of his mother who had also died of cancer. No matter how we interpret this passage, one thing is clear: it is a portrait of a highly disturbed adolescent. And in order to understand more fully Merton's description of his young self, we as readers must step back and consider who is writing this passage. Is Merton describing himself as he really was as a young man, or is Merton involved in a projection of a self-image he still has yet to come to terms with as an adult, now a monk in a Trappist monastery? Is he, in fact, projecting his shadow?

When Merton's father died, there was no atomic bomb, and the world had yet to employ the poison gas chambers where millions of Jews and others died. The year is 1931. We must, therefore, carefully examine and question Merton's description of himself as a great sinner, for every time he describes himself as such, he may be involved in shadow projection.

In the spring of 1932, Merton returned from a walking tour of Germany to his English prep school Oakham. He cut short his vacation because of an infected toe. On return to school he also developed an infected tooth. His body was full of poisonous gangrene. He had the school doctor pull the tooth. But he got sicker and was put in the infirmary where his health failed to improve. His doctor lanced a hole in his gum to drain the infection. Merton describes his mouth as "full of filth." He thought, "I have blood poisoning." Weary, in pain, filled with self-disgust, he writes,

> But I now lay on this bed, full of gangrene, and my soul was rotten with the corruption of my sins. And I did not even care whether I died or lived.[10]

He felt the presence of death; then he welcomed it, "Come on, I don't care.... If I have to die—what of it? What do I care? Let me die, then, and I am finished."[11] Eventually Merton informed his doctor that he also had an infected toe which he had developed in Germany. The toe was so full of gangrene that Merton almost lost it. Why the delay in informing his doctor? Was Merton punishing himself for his father's death, his mother's? Was he suicidal? And what, we ask, could be the sins to cause such self-disgust in one so young? Close reading of his autobiography reveals that his "sins" were those of any other young man: drinking, rowdy behavior, reading risque novels, flirtation with girls, all typical rites of passage for most young men.

For one of the causes of such self-hatred we must go back to his early childhood. Merton's mother had high standards for her son. She watched his every movement, she recorded his first words in "Tom's Book." She took charge of his education, well aware of all the new theories. Once, when she was trying to teach her son to spell, the five year old kept spelling "which" without the first "h." She sent him off to bed as punishment. Merton remembered thinking to himself, "What do they think I am, anyway?" At an early age perfection had been held up to him as an ideal, and when there occurred failure to reach the ideal, there was punishment. It is likely that his mother's perfectionist expectations, when imposed upon him, created in the child a conflict between what he was and what he should be. It is significant that Merton includes this childhood "failure" in his autobiography written twenty-five years after the event. And if as a teen-ager Merton felt a failure, as indicated by his description of himself after his father's death, then it is not hard to understand that he would punish himself by not revealing to his doctor information about his infected foot, the real cause of his blood poisoning. Nor would it be difficult to understand that he wanted to die. A young man unable to love himself because he thinks he is "rotten," full of malignity, might, indeed, welcome death as a release.

Merton had become "the thing a person has no wish to be." He had identified himself with his shadow, a lopsided psychological state that refuses to accept the good that is within oneself. It would take many years for Merton to accept himself, to integrate his shadow into consciousness. Merton's biographer Monica Furlong writes:

> Perhaps if his memories of Ruth (Merton) had been warmer, more satisfying, he might have been able to carry a different kind of confidence into adult life. She undoubtedly loved him and cared for him to the best of her ability, but there is always a faint bitterness in his references to her; she seemed critical, pedagogic, "severe," measuring him all the time against some standard that seemed unattainable, leaving him with a sour taste of failure, and of being inadequate.[12]

If the loss of one parent is traumatic, what can we say about the loss of both parents? Much of Merton's early adult life became a search for a home he had lost too soon. He was the modern, alienated young man without roots, a member of the lost generation. In 1966, looking back over his life, Merton laments "what a desperate, despairing childhood I had around the ages of seven—nine—ten."[13] And his adolescence fared not much better.

During his three and a half years at Oakham (1929-1933), Merton was an excellent student. Gifted in languages, he read Moliere, Racine, Balzac, Hugo, Goethe, and Schiller. He also enjoyed reading modern novelists such as Gide, Dos Passos, Hemingway, Lawrence, and Jules Romain. His essay on the modern fictional hero won him the Bailey English Prize. With his father dead, Merton turned more and more to fictional protagonists as his exemplars of contemporary behavior. Dr. Tom Bennet, appointed as Merton's guardian, encouraged such sophisticated reading; little did he know how closely Merton would emulate modern fictional heroes.

In December of 1933, when Merton was seventeen years old, he won a scholarship to Clare College, Cambridge. The day after his birthday, January 31, 1934, he embarked on a vacation to Italy, a journey that would change him forever.

Although he was a tourist, Merton describes himself in his autobiography as a pilgrim in Italy. Unaware of it at the time, he truly was a pilgrim in the original meaning of the word, one who visits religious shrines. In Roman churches he was fascinated with Byzantine mosaics, finding them not only beautiful, but also powerfully spiritual. These huge icons of Christ overwhelmed him, jerked him out of himself to the point that for the first time in his life he wanted and needed to know "who this Person was that men called Christ." He eagerly went from church to church to find mosaics and stained glass windows: Saints Cosmas and Damian, Santa Maria Maggiore, Santa Sabina, the Lateran, Santa Costanza, St. Prudenziana, and St. Praxeds.

In the beginning, it was the beauty of these mosaics that captured him. That beauty can serve as a bridge to the divine is supported by the French mystic, Simone Weil, whom Merton came to admire later in his life. Weil writes,

> In everything which gives us the pure, authentic feeling of beauty there is, as it were, an incarnation of God in the world, and it is indicated in beauty.[14]

Mesmerized by the spiritual power of Christian iconography, Merton haunted these old Roman churches and their treasures. To understand them and to learn more about their subject, Jesus Christ, Merton purchased a Vulgate Bible which he immediately proceeded to read. Thus for Merton, the aesthetic and the spiritual experience became one. Later in his life, sounding much like Simone Weil, Merton credits art as a spiritual force in our lives,

> Art enables us to find ourselves and lose ourselves at the same time. The mind that responds to the intellectual or spiritual values that lie hidden in a poem, a painting or a piece of music, discovers a spiritual vitality that lifts it above itself, takes it our of itself, and makes it present to itself on a level of being that it did not know it could ever achieve.[15]

From a Jungian perspective, Merton is well launched upon his journey to wholeness: he is obviously obeying his religious impulse, he seeks a life of meaning. But this stage of individuation is, however, still superficial. Gazing at artistic renditions of Christ outside oneself or reading about him is not the same as knowing the Christ within. Merton must more deeply enter these spiritual waters; he must, in short, be reborn by the water of baptism, still a long way off.

Merton's favorite shrine in Rome was St. Peter in Chains. He says he identified with St. Peter because he knew in his depths that he himself was chained by his own sins. It was, however, his own shadow that was in chains. Afraid to free his shadow, to permit its presence into his consciousness, he writes that his chains were "far heavier and more terrible than ever were his (Peter's)." There is an unhealthy boasting here, but this is an accurate description of the state of mind of a person whose ego represses his shadow into the darkness of the unconscious. His boasting about being a great sinner also focuses our attention on one glaring fact: his ego is still very much in control, suggesting his secret pride in being a greater sinner than St. Peter.

In a Roman hotel room Merton's shadow made its most alarming bid for recognition and integration:

> I was in my room. It was night. The light was on. Suddenly it seemed to me that Father, who had now been dead more than a year, was there with me. The sense of his presence was as vivid and as real and as startling as if he had touched my arm or spoken to me. The whole thing passed in a flash, but in that flash, instantly I was overwhelmed with a sudden and profound insight into the misery and corruption of my soul, and I was pierced deeply with a light that made me realize something of the condition I was in, and I was filled with horror at what I saw, and my whole being rose up in revolt against what was within me, and my soul desired escape and liberation and freedom from all this with an intensity and urgency unlike anything I had ever known before. And now I think for the first time in my whole life I really began to pray.[16]

As a Christian would be terrified by an encounter with the Devil, young Merton recoils at his awareness of his shadow. His reaction is a familiar one: who is not afraid to face the dark side of one's personality? Many people hide from their shadow either behind their personae or their projections, seeing the splinter in their neighbor's eye but rarely the plank in their own.

Merton is unnerved; he turns to prayer because he knows he needs the assistance of a higher power in facing the presence of his dark side. He needs the Self, the unifying force of the psyche symbolically represented by his father who, as previously mentioned, drew Byzantine faces on his deathbed, icons similar to the Byzantine mosaics that fascinated Merton in Rome. His father's death was a wounding of the personality, initiating Merton's entry upon the inner journey, urging him to consciously come to terms with his own inner center, his Self. He had been called to wholeness.

The Byzantine mosaics of Rome prepared Merton for this encounter with his shadow now crying for attention, for acceptance, for forgiveness, for integration. At this time Merton had the opportunity to experience another kind of death, the death of his personality dominated by the ego. If only Merton had surrendered his pride and embraced his shadow, he would have saved himself from many years of spiritual anguish, but he was not ready.

He writes, "I was filled with horror at what I saw, and my whole being rose up in revolt against what was within me."[17] Merton cannot accept his imperfect self, he still perceives himself in duality: the good me and the bad me. Jung suffered the same kind of duality, dividing himself into Personality 1 and 2. He has yet, as Jung would say, to *realize* his shadow. Such realization allows a person to achieve a reconciliation of opposites that accepts both the good and bad within oneself.

Of course, we might ask how it is possible for a teen-ager such as Merton to be horrified by his life. How is it possible for him to say "Did I not know that my own sins were enough to have destroyed the whole of England and Germany?" There is insufficient evidence in his autobiography to prove he was as evil as, for example, a Mister Kurtz who, as he approaches his death, cries, "the horror, the horror" —and rightfully so, for Kurtz truly lived a life of ruthless brutality. But Merton's autobiography offers us no evidence that he was a cruel young man. At this stage of his life he was most likely still a virgin, so he certainly could not have been terribly promiscuous. He was no saint, but he was not a great sinner either. A possible answer to this puzzle is offered by Esther Harding who says about such a self-image as Merton's:

> It represents a kind of "specialness" which manifests itself in a negative form, so that the one who suffers from it does not see that underlying the sense of humiliations and inferiority is an unconscious egotism and arrogance which says: Ordinary people may do these things but I am really so superior that in me they are sin.[18]

This manifestation of an unconscious egotism that sets oneself higher than other individuals by creating a hierarchy of sinners is certainly unhealthy, but paradoxically it is an important stage in Merton's individuation. Merton would eventually realize that the ego is not the center of the psyche but the Self which is the Christ, a realization that would lead him into the Catholic church.

As we shall see, Merton's shadow does not disappear when he converts to Christianity; nor does it disappear because he becomes a Trappist. It was for a short time quieted. In time he would learn that there is no escape (for which he prayed in his hotel room) from the shadow which is, as Jung says, an integral part of one's psyche. Jung uses the analogy of painting to illustrate his idea: without shadow and light there can be no painting because it is from the play of light and shadow that beauty emerges. So too with people: it is from the play of opposites that reside in every person that the beauty of the human soul emerges.

In the meantime, Merton avoided facing his shadow by projecting it onto the world in general (*contemptus mundi*), and specifically onto cities such as Cambridge, London, and New York; cities that became for Merton symbols of sin and corruption.

Why did it take Merton so long to come to terms with his shadow? Why couldn't he simply forgive himself, become friends with his shadow? Jung counsels:

> Simple things are always the most difficult. In actual life it requires the greatest art to be simple, and so, acceptance of oneself is the essence of the moral problem and the acid test of one's whole outlook on life. That I feed the beggar, that I forgive an insult, that I love my enemy in the name of Christ—all these are undoubtedly great virtues. What I do unto the least of my brethren, that I do unto to Christ. But what if I should discover that the least amongst them all, the poorest of all beggars, the most impudent of all offenders, yea, the very fiend himself—that these are within me, and that I myself stand in need of the alms of my own kindness, that I myself am the enemy who must be loved—what then?
>
> We hide from the world, we deny ever having met this least among the lowly in ourselves, and had it been God himself who drew near to us in this despicable form, we should have denied him a thousand times before a single cock had crowed.[19]

And so like Peter's denial of Christ, Merton would continue to deny his shadow integration, deny the archetypal Self. Not until the Louisville Vision in 1958 will we see noticeable progress in Merton's taking back his shadow projections, finally resulting in the disappearance of his too long-held *contemptus mundi*.

TWO

CAMBRIDGE UNIVERSITY: OBJECT OF SHADOW PROJECTION

A person's hatred is always concentrated on the thing that makes him conscious of his bad qualities.[1]

In the fall of 1933 Merton arrived at the university city of Cambridge, famous for the beauty of its quads, the marshes, and the river Cam. King's Chapel with its fan vaulting is one of the most exquisite churches in Christendom. Merton, however, saw none of Cambridge's beauty, for him it was hell on earth. He describes Cambridge:

> Perhaps to you the atmosphere of Cambridge is neither dark nor sinister. Perhaps you were never there except in May. You never saw anything but the thin Spring sun half veiled in the mists and blossoms of the gardens along the Backs, smiling on the lavender bricks and stones of Trinity and St. John's, or my own college Clare.
>
> I am even willing to admit that some people might live there for three years, or even a lifetime, so protected that they never sense the sweet stench of corruption that is all around them—the keen, thin

scent of decay that pervades everything and accuses with a terrible accusation the superficial youthfulness, the abounding undergraduate noise that fills those ancient buildings. But for me, with my blind appetites, it was impossible that I should not rush in and take a huge bite of this rotten fruit. The bitter taste is still with me after not a few years.[2]

This is a far cry from the poetic description of Oakham, Merton's public school:

In the autumn of 1929 I went to Oakham. There was something very pleasant and peaceful about the atmosphere of this little market town, with its school and its old fourteenth century church with the grey spire, rising in the middle of a wide Midland vale.[3]

Attention should be given to Merton's diction in describing Cambridge. Language like "dark" and "sinister" and "stench of corruption" and "scent of decay" echo the language of the first sections of Dante's *Divine Comedy*, specifically the first two cantos, the "Inferno" and "Purgatorio," which Merton studied at Clare College. This introduction to Dante, he says, was "the greatest grace in the positive order that I got out of Cambridge."[4]

What happened between 1929-1933 to transform so drastically Merton's impressions of England, a land he hitherto had loved?

Five profound experiences account for Merton's negative view of England in general and Cambridge in particular. They are the death of his father (1931), his experience of his shadow in a Roman hotel room (1933), the death of his beloved Aunt Maud (1933), his problems with sexuality, and a bizarre experience at a party (November 14, 1933).

Merton says that he took "a huge bite of this rotten fruit," the rotten fruit being Cambridge University. In October of 1933 when Merton arrived there, Cambridge certainly was no more evil than any other college town or city in England or for that matter anywhere. Merton unconsciously employs this university town as a scapegoat for his feelings of sin and guilt. He indicts not only England, but all of Europe:

> But it seemed to me that there was some kind of subtle poison in Europe, something that corrupted me, something the very thought and scent of which sickened me, repelled me. What was it? Some kind of a moral fungus, the spores of which floated in that damp air, in that foggy and half-lighted darkness.[5]

Notice Merton's use of passive verbs: he *is* "corrupted," "sickened," and "repelled" by something outside himself, a classic example of shadow projection. Unwilling to claim his shadow, Merton projects it onto everything around him. He also views himself as a victim of this evil world: he *is* corrupted; therefore, *he* is not responsible. In his immaturity he has failed to grasp the truth that fault lies not in anything outside ourselves, "not in our stars but in ourselves."

The corruption, the poison, the moral fungus, the fog, the damp air, the half-lighted darkness—all these images suggest evil and at the same time are symbolic of the unconscious. Paradoxically, from this compost can come great good if it is claimed, worked, and integrated into consciousness. Jung reiterates the Janus-faced nature of the unconscious:

> The unconscious is not just evil by nature, it is also the source of the highest good: not only dark but also

41

light, not only bestial, semi-human and demonic but superhuman, spiritual, and, in the classical sense of the world, "divine."[6]

The first event to cloud Merton's vision of Cambridge occurred with Owen Merton's death on January 18, 1931, expelling Merton from youth's Garden of Eden forever. It thrust the young man on his search for life's meaning. Although his father's death shut the doors of the Garden of Eden behind him, it opened before him the gates of the unconscious mind, revealing especially his shadow through various guises of shame, guilt, and self-disgust. And although all this was harrowing for the young man (Merton names this chapter of his autobiography "The Harrowing of Hell") it is, as we shall see, a blessing in disguise.

Death, naturally, calls into question the meaning of life. Death is all around us, and the young Merton was already too acquainted with the night of death, having lost both his mother and father before his sixteenth birthday. But this night of suffering would be a fertile seedbed of growth for Merton because he would commit himself to an exploration of life and death that would necessitate his cultivation of the inward gaze which would lead him into the depths of his own psyche where lie the divine symbols of wholeness/holiness.

The second experience to influence Merton's perception of Cambridge was his prior encounter with his shadow in his Roman hotel room. This also awakened in the young Merton his need for God. The day after his experience in the Roman hotel room, Merton found his way to the Dominican church Santa Sabina where he prayed, "with all the belief I had in me, the Our Father."[7]

Little did he know at the time that prayer would some day become his vocation.

His new found religious fervor, however, was short-lived. Before beginning his academic life at Cambridge, he returned to America to visit his grandparents. His spiritual intentions faded next to America's capital of "bigness and gaudiness and noisiness and frank animality and vulgarity of American paganism"—New York.

The third event which jaundiced Merton's view of Cambridge was the death in England of his beloved Aunt Maud in November of 1933. She was his last link to his youth. His account of her burial is moving:

> They committed the thin body of my poor Victorian angel to the clay of Ealing, and buried my childhood with her. In an obscure, half-conscious way I realized this and was appalled. She it was who presided in a certain sense over my most innocent days. And now I saw those days buried with her in the ground.[8]

It was through her eyes that he first fell in love with England:

> Pretty country churches, the quiet villages, the elm trees along the common where the cricketers wait in white while the bowler pensively paces out of a rum for himself behind the wicket. The huge white clouds that sail over Sussex, the bell-charmed spires of the ancient county towns, the cathedral closes full of trees, the deaneries that ring with rooks.[9]

Many of the images of this passage have a religious connotation: churches, spires, cathedral closes, and deaneries. The transition from this kind of imagery to that of his description of Cambridge suggests not so much the landscape of England as it does the landscape of Merton's soul. Innocence is lost forever; he must find his way in the world, alone.

After his aunt's death, Merton's life at Cambridge became a wild one of drinking, partying, and girl chasing. His biographer Michael Mott suggests that it is likely that at Cambridge Merton lost his virginity, and this loss brings us to the matter of Merton's erotic life.[10]

His friends colorfully describe Merton's lifestyle at Cambridge by remarking "he went off the rails," he was a "ship without an anchor," he "mucked with the wrong set," he went "wenching and drinking," "debauchery is not too strong a word" for his behavior.[11] And while he was at Cambridge, he fathered a child—a fact not revealed in his published autobiography. Merton's guardian Tom Bennet was not very sympathetic or sensitive in his treatment of the fatherless young man. Bennet summoned Merton to his London office. He kept Merton waiting for an hour and a half. The actual meeting between the two took less than twenty minutes, the most painful and distressing time the young man ever lived through. Merton writhed in shame as he tried to explain to his guardian that he was sorry for his behavior and that he had not intended to hurt anyone. Monica Furlong writes of this interview:

> Merton's orphaned state had never stood him in worse stead, for while his own parents, if they had been alive, might have demurred at his youthful rakishness and demanded an explanation, it is unlikely that they would have set up the inquiry in quite so painful and magisterial a way or with so little feeling for his youth and sensitivity. In fact, of course, Bennet's attack seemed particularly unjust because

Merton was however naively, attempting to follow the pattern of being "the man of the world" that he believed Bennet had indicated to him, following the sexual mores of writers such as Hemingway and Lawrence, whom Bennet admired.[12]

Merton returned to Cambridge, but his class attendance was sporadic. He managed to achieve only a second in the Modern Language Tripos, but nevertheless he planned to continue his education at Clare College in the fall of 1934. But while in America on a visit to his maternal grandparents, he received a letter from his guardian suggesting he give up the idea of entering the British Diplomatic service. Bennet told him outright that it would be better for him to remain in America, a suggestion Merton readily embraced:

> The thought that I was no longer obliged to go back into those damp and fetid mists filled me with an immense relief—a relief that far overbalanced the pain of my injured pride, the shame of comparative failure.[13]

If his experience in his Roman hotel room revealed to Merton the dimensions of his shadow, then it seems that at Cambridge he tried to prove to himself and others that he, indeed, was a terrible sinner. From a Jungian perspective, we can understand his actions: his ego was in its last fierce battle to maintain control of his psyche. If we wish to be generous in our understanding of the young Merton, we could simply identify his actions with not uncommon adolescent rites of passage. There are sufficient number of English autobiographies chronicling the wild university life prevalent at England's most famous universities, Oxford and

Cambridge, including the fiction and non-fiction of another famous Catholic convert Evelyn Waugh, an Oxford student.

From another perspective we could say there was good in his "sins," for where sin abides, grace abounds (see Romans 5:20).

Jung says the journey to wholeness requires the thorn in the flesh:

> There is no light without shadow and no psychic wholeness without imperfection. To round itself out, life calls not for perfection but for completeness; and for this the "thorn in the flesh" is needed, the suffering of defects without which there is no progress and no ascent.[14]

Thus, Merton had to suffer the thorns of the flesh; it was a necessary rite of passage. He had to journey through the hell of desire. He had to experience instinctual life, an integral part of the journey to wholeness. He had to accept the reality of his body as well as his soul: both have their demands and somehow reconciliation between them must be achieved. At Cambridge he was, of course, too young to realize these truths; he would learn, like most people, through the painful way of experience.

Michael Mott also suggests another reason for Merton's jaundiced view of Cambridge. He gives an account of a party Merton attended where a mock crucifixion was re-enacted, possibly with Merton playing the role of Christ. This event appears in Merton's unpublished novel *The Labyrinth*, written in 1939. Many years later, Merton's friend and agent Naomi Burton Stone, one day noticed a scar on the palm of his right hand. When she asked him about it, Merton awkwardly joked it was his "stigmata."[15]

In November of 1934 Merton sailed from Southhampton for America, never to see England again. When he summarized his life in England, he characteristically tended to blame England or rather the world in general for the kind of person he turned out to be:

> I was something that had been spawned by selfishness and irresponsibility of the materialistic century in which I lived. However, what I did not see was that my own age and class only had an accidental part to play in this. They gave me egoism and pride and my other sins a peculiar character of weak and supercilious flippancy proper to this particular century: but that was only on the surface. Underneath, it was the same old story of greed and lust and self-love, of the three concupiscences bred in the rich, rotted undergrowth of what is technically called "the world" in every age, in every class.[16]

Later on in his autobiography he compares the twentieth century to pagan Rome. He sounds very much like Shakespeare's Hamlet for whom Denmark was an unweeded garden. When Merton departed from England he was only nineteen years old, in the last stages of his adolescence. Theodore Roethke offers a succinct poetic description of this time of life:

> So much of adolescence is an ill-defined dying,
> An intolerable waiting,
> A longing for another place and time,
> Another condition.[17]

In America Merton would continue his inner journey, searching for psychic wholeness.

THREE

EXPERIMENTATION WITH PERSONAE

In a dark time the eye begins to see.[1]

On his return to America, Merton resided with his maternal grandparents in Douglaston, New York. Dr. Bennet settled Merton's paternity case out of court, arranging a financial settlement with the mother. To this day no one is certain about what happened to the mother and child. The rumor is that both were killed in the blitz.[2]

Certainly Merton's nineteenth year was one of the darkest periods of his life, and naturally, Merton welcomed Bennet's suggestion to remain in America where the young man could start over again. Merton says of his year at Cambridge:

> It did not take very much reflection on the year I had spent at Cambridge to show me that all my dreams of fantastic pleasures and delights were crazy and absurd, and that everything I had reached out for had turned to ashes in my hands, and that I myself, into the bargain, had turned out to be an extremely unpleasant sort of a person—vain, self-centered, dissolute, weak, irresolute, undisciplined, sensual, obscene and proud. I was a mess ... the sight of my own face in a mirror was enough to disgust me.[3]

The lengthy list of negative adjectives indicting himself is relentlessly harsh. Such a portrait of himself, it should be remembered, was written by a thirty-year-old monk recalling his youth, a monk projecting his shadow onto his image of himself as a young man. The young child, who was punished for not spelling the pronoun "which" correctly, had grown into a person quite adept with language, a person whose standards of behavior equaled, if not surpassed, those of his mother.

Although his life in Cambridge had been disastrous, Merton was still a fortunate person in that not many young men are given second chances when it comes to fathering children out of wedlock. He did not have to abandon his education, marry, and support his wife and child. Merton's social position, upper middle class because of his grandfather Sam Jenkins' money and influence, offered him a second chance. He, however, failed to transform himself as quickly as he might have.

In America, Merton's first psychological order of business was to decide upon which persona he would adopt in his new country. As suggested, Merton had the opportunity to be a different person, more responsible, more mature; he decided, to his later dismay, to retain in his repertoire of personae, masks which he should have left in England. In fact, Merton dabbles with so many personae that he, like the poet, could ask, "Which I is I?"[4]

In experimenting with too many masks, we may lose sight of who we really are, and if we identify too much with one particular mask, we may find ourselves doing things that are based on what that persona "should" do, think, and feel, all of which may also be predetermined by what we think others expect of us. Jung writes, "One could say, with a little exaggeration, that the persona is that which in reality one is not, but which oneself as well as others think one is."[5]

The vocational mask Merton hoped to adopt was that of journalist, and he was advised that a college degree would be helpful toward this end. He enrolled at Columbia University in February of 1935. He described Columbia as a refreshing change from Cambridge, "full of light and fresh air." Merton the student immediately immersed himself in a whirl of activity including, besides academic courses, parties, drinking, dating, sports, and pledging a fraternity. He also joined the literary magazine the *Jester* where he met people who would remain lifetime friends, notably Robert Lax and Ed Rice. He also worked for other campus publications: the yearbook, the *Spectator* and the *Columbia Review* where he met his future publisher Robert Giroux and the poet John Berryman. His political persona involved a brief flirtation with the Young Communist League, adopting the party name Frank Swift; but he was quickly disenchanted after attending only one meeting. In a short time, Merton was a big man on campus.

Socially Merton continued to wear the persona of rake, boasting to his friends at Columbia that he fathered a child in England. Thus, he would persist in activities which reinforced his persona of sexual athlete and heavy drinker, to the point that his college fraternity, dazzled by Merton's sybaritic lifestyle, often referred to him as "our Merty." How much of a rake Merton actually was, we perhaps may never know, but one thing is certain: Merton found himself just as unhappy and unfulfilled in America as he was in England. The one difference being, however, that at Columbia he had at least earned his B.A. and M.A. in English.

The vortex of activity and the death of his grandfather Sam Jenkins in November, 1936, brought Merton to the edge of nervous collapse. On a train going to New York City from Douglaston, Long Island, Merton suffered an attack of vertigo. As he made his way to the passageway between cars for fresh air, he had another attack almost plunging him to the railway tracks and certain death. He held on until he reached Penn Station, crossed the street, and checked himself into the Pennsylvania Hotel where he had a doctor examine him. The house doctor suggested immediate rest. Merton never forgot that day,

> I lay on the bed and I listened to the blood pounding rapidly inside my head. I could hardly keep my eyes closed. Yet I did not want to open them, either. I was afraid that if I even looked at the window, the strange spinning inside my head would begin again.
>
> That window! It was huge. It seemed to go right down to the floor. Maybe the force of gravity would draw the whole bed, with me on it, to the edge of that abyss, and spill me headlong into the emptiness.
>
> And far, far away in my mind was a little, dry, mocking voice that said: "What if you threw yourself out of the window...." I thought to myself: "I wonder if I am having a nervous breakdown?"[6]

This was not the first time he felt suicidal. Merton, it seems, created another mess out of his life even though he had accomplished what he set out to do, creating a big splash at Columbia. The Columbia yearbook was filled with pictures of him. He had friends, he was popular, he dated several young women. Academically he performed well above average. Although he was extremely unhappy, he rejected suicide. Shortly after his scary train ride, Merton was diagnosed with a severe case of gastritis, bordering on ulcers. His doctor prescribed medicine and put him on a special diet.

Today we know enough about psychosomatic illness to understand that Merton's physical problems were likely the result of his sick soul which he described as filled with "distress and anguish and fear"—the result of not having lived from his true center.

Around this same time, Merton suffered from another setback. He fell into a love affair that ended with his being so summarily rejected by a woman that he felt humiliated and wounded. He described his psychic state, "I was bleeding to death."

According to Jung people have not only a persona, an outward face which they present to the world, but they also have an inward face he calls the anima in males, the animus in females. A man's anima, if he is attentive to it, will assist him in achieving psychic wholeness and will help him to relate to people in the world. The same is true for the woman who is attentive to her animus. Describing the anima, Jung says:

> Every man carries within him the eternal image of the woman, not the image of this or that particular woman, but a definite feminine image. This image is fundamentally unconscious, an hereditary factor of primordial origin engraved in the living organic system of the man, an imprint or archetype of all the ancestral experiences of the female, a deposit, as it were, of all the impressions ever made by woman.... Since this image is unconscious, it is always unconsciously projected upon the person of the beloved, and is one of the chief reasons for passionate attraction or aversion.[7]

A young male child's initial projection of the anima is onto his mother. Later in life he will project his anima onto a woman, and if she accepts his projection, and he the projection of her animus, the dynamic of falling in love is likely.

If a male child undergoes a negative maternal experience, it may adversely affect his relationships with other women for the rest of his life. If a male child feels his projection of his anima is being rejected by his mother, then for the rest of his life he may distrust/fear all that is feminine—a distrust and fear which would include himself because he carries within him his own inner woman.

During his young adult life, Merton failed repeatedly to establish a lasting relationship with the opposite sex. Having lost his mother at such an early age, Merton may have unconsciously feared another abandonment by a woman, severing a relationship before it could hurt him. Thus no relationship had the chance to blossom into a healthy, nurturing one. Or it may have even been more complicated.

There is a poignant scene in Merton's childhood when he was delivered a letter from his mother informing the little boy that he would never see her again. On some level Merton may have felt that his mother rejected him. His relationship with his mother had not been particularly healthy, she was, as noted, severe, exacting, and distant with her child. Without too much difficulty, we perhaps can understand why Merton felt unlovable for much of his life. On the eve of his fiftieth birthday, Merton himself attempted to understand his problem with the opposite sex,

> I suppose I regret most my lack of love, my selfishness and glibness (covering a deep shyness and need for love) with girls who, after all, did love me, I think,

for a time. My great fault was my inability really, to believe it, and my efforts to get complete assurance and perfect fulfillment.[8]

Carl Jung experienced a similar problem. When he was three years old, he was temporarily separated from his ill mother. He was cared for by an aunt and a family maid. The separation from his mother, however, marked him for life. He writes that he was "deeply troubled ... from then on I always felt mistrustful when the word 'love' was spoken. The feeling I associated with 'woman' was for a long time that of innate unreliability."[9] If this was the result of Jung's temporary separation, what can we assume about Merton's permanent separation from his mother caused by death?

If Merton unconsciously felt women to be unreliable and imperfect, how would he be able to project his anima? He must somehow find a reliable woman, one who would accept him along with his shadow which, we must remember, made him feel miserable much of the time. We shall see that Merton's life would mysteriously fulfill T. S. Eliot's prophetic verse that the only hope of empty men is "the perpetual star" and "the multifoliate rose" — that is, Mary, mother of God, and God's church.

In the meantime, Merton must find the necessary guides to direct him through his hell of confusion, just as Virgil led Dante through hell to Beatrice. As Merton was spiritually inspired by art in Rome, he was similarly moved and influenced by great writers. That Merton would be inspired by writers is not surprising since he aspired to be one himself. The word, it seems, would dominate Merton's life. Jung says *Logos* (Greek for word) is a principle characteristic of men because it involves judgment and discrimination; he says: "Logos is essential reason. Each person, therefore, has his *own* Logos which connects him, ultimately, with meaning."[10]

Some of the writers from whom Merton sought meaning are Etienne Gilson, Aldous Huxley, William Blake, Jacques Maritain, and Gerard Manley Hopkins. Each of these artists offered to Merton some ray of insight that illuminated his way of conversion to Catholicism.

In February of 1937, walking past Scribner's Bookshop on Fifth Avenue, Merton noticed in its window Etienne Gilson's book *The Spirit of Medieval Philosophy*. He began to read it on the train home. When he observed that the book contained the church's stamp of approval with its *Nihil Obstat* ("nothing stands in the way") and *Imprimatur* ("let it be printed"), he was disgusted and wanted to throw the book out the train window. He felt he had been cheated and should have been warned that he was purchasing a Catholic book. Although he was capable of appreciating Catholic churches and Catholic art, Merton remained ambivalent about the Catholic church, perhaps the result of his grandfather's anti-Catholic bias. But now through this particular book he had the opportunity to read about the philosophical and theological foundation of Catholicism whose symmetry, beauty, and depth were as luminous and moving as the mosaics he fell in love with in Rome. For the first time he was introduced to a concept of God that was intellectually satisfying. According to Gilson, a Thomist, only God possesses the quality of *aseitas*: God is pure Being, existing always in, of, by itself. This concept, Merton says, was to "revolutionize my whole life."

Not long after reading Gilson, Merton desired to go to church, and he began to attend the Episcopal Church Zion in Douglaston where his father once played the organ.

Aldous Huxley's book of essays *Ends and Means* introduced Merton to two spiritual ways: asceticism and mysticism. Merton was attracted to asceticism perhaps because he had been so much a victim of the desires of the flesh. He was also drawn to the possibility of detachment and discipline as a means of liberating himself from desire so that the real self could be experienced. Such an idea also caused another "revolution" in his mind. The world of mysticism opened up to Merton the possibility of experiencing God in this life. Huxley wrote at length about such Catholic mystics as Teresa of Avila, John of the Cross, and Eckhart. They would in the near future exert a far-reaching influence on Merton, one that would last a lifetime. Huxley also stimulated Merton's interest in Buddhism, an interest that would blossom in the 1960s.

William Blake was a poet whom Merton grew to love; he wrote his master's thesis on Blake. Blake's poetry dealt with the profound problem of good and evil, the role of humanity in a corrupt world, and the suppression of desire and its expression. Like Merton, Blake was imbued with a similar *contemptus mundi*. In addition to being a poet, Blake was a mystic, an artist, and an admirer of Dante. Merton saw him as a spiritual brother. Although non-Catholic, Blake described Catholicism as the only religion that really taught God's love and God's forgiveness: two things for which Merton hungered.

Merton's study of Blake became a joy and a grace, "But, oh, what a thing it was to live in contact with the genius and holiness of William Blake that year, that summer, writing my thesis."[11] Blake's influence was so substantial that the name of the first chapter of Merton's most popular book, *Seeds of Contemplation* is taken from Blake, "Everything that is, is Holy."

While writing his master's thesis, Merton read another book, Jacques Maritain's *Art and Scholasticism* which further intrigued him with Catholicism. Merton discovered in Maritain a "sane conception of virtue—without which there can be no happiness, because virtues are precisely the powers by which we can come to acquire happiness: without them, there can be no joy."[12]

By the beginning of September 1938, the groundwork for Merton's conversion was more or less complete. Merton says it took an little more than a year and a half from the time he read Gilson to bring him from an "atheist," as he considered himself to be, to being a person open to the immense range and possibility of religious experience. Thus Merton was ready and ripe for conversion. He had developed an appreciation of Catholic theology, an attraction to asceticism and mysticism, he craved love and forgiveness, and he possessed a desire for virtue. All that was missing was a exemplar to inspire him.

The final writer to influence Merton was Gerard Manley Hopkins. Merton and Hopkins also had much in common. Both were non-Catholic and suspicious of Catholicism, both were intellectuals, both were poets, and both were attracted to the idea of perfection. We can imagine Merton reading and being moved by Hopkins' poem "The Habit of Perfection," whose opening verse became the title of the English version of Merton's autobiography *Elected Silence*.

On an October day in 1938, Merton was reading G. F. Lahey's biography of Gerard Manley Hopkins. When he arrived at the section where Hopkins finally decided to seek Newman's help to convert to Catholicism, Merton impulsively got up and walked to Corpus Christi Church near Columbia and informed Father Ford he wanted to be accepted into the Catholic church.

On November 16, 1938 Merton was baptized. He had finally found a worthy recipient for his anima projection, Holy Mother Church. Through baptism Merton was reborn as a Christian; on that day he made his first communion. Baptism wiped away his sins of a lifetime. His conversion solved his anima problem by finding a bride in the church and by temporarily silencing his shadow.

Fascinated with the healing power of water (he lived near water all his life), Jung understood the profound significance of baptism:

> Baptism endows the human being with a unique soul ... the idea of baptism lifts a man out of his archaic identification with the world and changes him into a being who stands above it. The fact that mankind has risen to the level of this idea is baptism in the deepest sense, for it means the birth of spiritual man who transcends nature.[13]

Through baptism Merton became a man who had at last found his soul. Shortly after his conversion, Merton began attending Mass on a regular basis. This became his most important spiritual exercise, one which would never wane.

Jung, though not a Catholic, had a deep, abiding respect for the mystery of the Mass:

> The Mass is an extramundane and extratemporal act in which Christ is sacrificed and then resurrected in the transformed substances; and this rite of his sacrificial death is not a repetition of the historical event but the original, unique and eternal act. The experience of the Mass is therefore a participation in the transcendence of life, which overcomes all bounds of space and time.[14]

Jung offers a psychological interpretation of the Mass in his essay "Transformation Symbolism in the Mass." For Jung the Mass symbolizes the sacrifice of the ego to the Self. When the ego is sacrificed, the individual is infused with Christ consciousness. As he looked at the symbolism of the Mass as he knew it, prior to Vatican II, Jung found many **mandalas** (symbols of wholeness). Jung believed that through the mandalas of the host, the patten, the purificator, the pall, the chalice veil, the chalice and the altar, the priest created a spiritual/psychological mandala with Christ as the center. Thus the Mass is symbolic of the unfolding of the flower of individuation: I (ego) decreases that Christ (Self) may increase.

While visiting Cuba in April of 1940, Merton attended a Mass which became one of the most **numinous** experiences of his life, equal to that of the Louisville Vision (March 18, 1958) and the Polonnaruwa Buddhas (December 2, 1968).

In 1937, Jung described the *numinosum,*

> A dynamic agency or effect not caused by an arbitrary act of will. On the contrary, it seizes and

controls the human subject, who is always rather its victim than its creator. The *numinosum*—whatever its cause may be—is an experience of the subject independent of his will.... The *numinosum* is either a quality belonging to a visible object or the influence of an invisible presence that causes a peculiar alteration of consciousness.[15]

Like grace, the numinous is a gift, in addition to being an experience of tremendously compelling force: "it is a confrontation with a force that implies a not-yet-disclosed, attractive and fateful meaning."[16] Such impressive happenings go under other names: "peak experience," "moment of being," "epiphany," "timeless moment," and "mystical experience." What they all have in common is that language fails to convey its stunning effects. William James in *Varieties of Religious Experience* describes such occurrences as ineffable.

Prior to his numinous Mass, Merton intensely prayed to the Blessed Mother. He found his way into many cool, dark Cuban churches where he prayed to the Virgin Mary "full of miracle and pathos and clad in silks and black velvet, throned high above the high altars." His favorite devotion was to *La Soledad*, Our Lady of Solitude. At the Basilica of Our Lady of Cobre he prayed "There you are, *Caridad del Cobre*! It is you that I have come to see." After this visit Merton wrote what he describes as his first "real" poem, "Song for Our Lady of Cobre."

Returning to Havana, Merton attended Sunday Mass at St. Francis Church. Merton offers two accounts of his experience: one appears in *The Secular Journal* (April, 1940), the other in *The Seven Storey Mountain*. The following is from his autobiography,

It came time for the Consecration. The priest raised the Host, then he raised the chalice. When he put the chalice down on the altar, suddenly a Friar in his brown robe and white cord stood up in front of the children, and all at once the voices of the children burst out:

"*Creo en Dios* ...."

"I believe in God the Father Almighty, the creator of heaven and earth...."

The Creed. But that cry, "*Creo en Dios!*" It was loud, and bright, and sudden, and glad, and triumphant; it was a good big shout, that came from all those Cuban children, a joyous affirmation of faith.

Then, as sudden as the shout and as definite, and a thousand times more bright, there formed in my mind an awareness, an awareness, an understanding, a realization of what had just taken place on the altar, at the Consecration: a realization of God made present by the words of Consecration in a way that made him belong to me.

And yet the thing that struck me most of all was that this light was in a certain sense "ordinary"—it was a light (and this most of all was what took my breath away) that was offered to all, to everybody, and there was nothing fancy or strange about it. It was the light of faith deepened and reduced to an extreme and sudden obviousness.

It was as if I had been suddenly illuminated by being blinded by the manifestation of God's presence.... It lasted only a moment: but it left a breathless joy and a clean peace and happiness that stayed for hours and it was something I have never forgotten.[17]

This experience reveals the Self had momentarily broken through the bonds and controls of Merton's ego so that he might experience the Self. For a brief moment he loses himself, experiencing Christ's promise, "Those who lose their life for my sake will find it" (Mt 16:25). Merton was so awed by what happened to him that he encountered great difficulty in writing about it. He says, "it disarmed all images, all metaphors, and cut through the whole skein of species and phantasms with which we naturally do our thinking." [18] He finally settled for the image of light to convey his experience, likely the influence of his close reading of Dante, his favorite poet. Dante saw the kingdom as a dazzling rose of light, a light that transformed him forever,

> Whoever sees that light is soon made such
> that it would be impossible for him
> to set that Light aside for other sight. [19]

The invasion of light is a common one in spiritual accounts. Augustine records his mystical experience in *Confessions*: "You shone upon me, your radiance enveloped me, you put my blindness to flight."

Merton's desire to be a priest intensified. He had applied for acceptance into the Franciscan order. Teaching English at St. Bonaventure's, a Franciscan college, he was already imagining himself as a Franciscan monk who would one day celebrate Mass in the brown robe and leather sandals as worn by the followers of St. Francis. Then Merton suffered a case of religious scrupulosity and felt compelled to inform the Franciscans of his past, including his fathering a child. When the order learned of this, they asked him to withdraw his application. It was a terrible blow to Merton.

Why did Merton succumb to a compulsion to reveal his shady past to the Franciscans? He had already confessed his past and received absolution, everything had been wiped clean. It is likely that Merton had not forgiven himself, perhaps he was unconsciously punishing himself. By revealing his past to the Franciscans, he denied himself his most intense desire, to be a priest. The rejection depressed him. He says, "It seemed to me that I was now excluded from the priesthood forever." And he wept over this.

His friend Dan Walsh informed Merton of the Trappist monastery in Kentucky, recommending that Merton go on retreat there. Merton fell in love with the Abbey of Gethsemani, saying, "This is the center of America." Back at St. Bonaventure's he talked to one of the friars, asking him if fathering a child were an insurmountable obstacle to becoming a priest. Father Philotheus suggested it should not be an impediment. Merton immediately wrote to Gethsemani.

On December 10, 1941 Merton arrived at the gates of the Abbey of Our Lady of Gethsemani where he asked entry into the Trappist order. He was accepted as a postulant; he was twenty-seven years old.

As he entered the monastery gate, he would pass under a statue of Mary as Our Lady of Victory, below which was the salutation, "Peace."

FOUR

FALSE SELF AND TRUE SELF

There is only one true flight from the world; it is not an escape from conflict, anguish and suffering, but the flight from disunity and separation, to unity and peace in the love of other men.[1]

When Merton entered Gethsemani on December 10, 1941 he stepped back in time, into eleventh century medieval monastic life. Located in the remote hills of Kentucky, a harsh country hot in summer and cold in winter, Gethsemani was the first Cistercian foundation in America, established in 1849.

Life at Gethsemani was lived according to the Rule of St. Benedict, a rigorous, austere life based on manual labor and prayer known as *lectio divina*, requiring hours of communal worship. Monks rose at 2 a.m. for Vigils; they retired after Compline at 7 p.m. They wore black and white habits and cowl in which they worked and slept. Monks resided in one long dormitory which was divided by partitions into cells with a curtain as a door, permitting little privacy. Each cell contained one wooden bed covered with a straw mattress, a crucifix and a stoup of holy water hung on the wall. Their diet was vegetarian; meat, fish, and eggs were forbidden. During Advent and Lent the monks fasted.

Merton enthusiastically embraced this ascetic, penitential lifestyle. With an ever present sense of guilt about his sinful past, he relished such a life which, he believed, would purge him and transform him into a saint, the true goal, he believed, of every Catholic. Yet he soon discovered that the complete transformation that he expected such a life to effect never materialized. Merton was still very much himself, a divided man who had yet to learn the wisdom of self-acceptance, a man/monk still in search of the *ignis fatuus* of perfection.

He admits both in his autobiography and in his journal *The Sign of Jonas* that he was followed into Gethsemani by his writer-self. He says: "This shadow, this double, this writer ... had followed me into the cloister."[2] It is interesting that Merton would employ the word "shadow" to describe this aspect of himself which he had hoped would disappear; he would soon discover it impossible to give up *everything*, his intense desire when he entered the Trappists. In addition to his double, Merton brought with him into Gethsemani his shadow (in a Jungian sense), along with its concomitant *contemptus mundi*, which also refused to disappear.

Fortunately his abbot Dom Frederic Dunne saw that Merton was a born writer and wisely concluded that to permit the young monk to repress this integral part of his personality would be wasteful and perhaps psychologically harmful. He therefore encouraged Merton to write. Thus even in the first years of his monastic life Merton continued to be a writer. Although he did perform his fair share of manual labor, this along with his writing proved too strenuous, bringing him close to physical collapse. Concerned about Merton's health, the abbot freed him from physical work to allow him to pursue a more intellectual life, at the same time assigning him several writing projects involving Cistercian history and hagiography. Around 1944 he also encouraged Merton to proceed with his plan to write his autobiography. By October, 1946, Merton had sent his manuscript of *The Seven Storey Mountain* to his agent Naomi Burton. In December 1946 he began his journal to be published as *The Sign of Jonas* (1953), and in 1947 he began his book of spiritual insights, *Seeds of Contemplation* (1949). At the same time he was writing a history of monasticism, *The Waters of Siloe* (1949). As incredible as it may sound, he was also writing a commentary on the mysticism of St. John of the Cross (1951).

Seeds of Contemplation was published one year after *The Seven Storey Mountain*. On the heels of a bestseller, it too was an enormous success, astonishing Merton who wrote to a friend that his little book on contemplation sold well even in Hollywood!

America, it seems, was ready for such a book. Many Americans, both Catholic and Protestant, were ready to embark on the interior journey. America had experienced the horrors of World War II; it had entered the atomic age; it was aware of the horrors of Nagasaki and Hiroshima. The horrific fact that man had unleashed a destructive force powerful enough to destroy the world lingered in the air. The forties had truly become the Age of Anxiety, on the verge of another war, the Cold War. Merton appeared on the literary scene at the right time, and America was ripe for his spiritual message. It is, then, not surprising that in the postwar years Gethsemani's population doubled. Many American men, who had suffered the agonies of war and had seen the incredible carnage of the death camps, now realized that only the eternal verities mattered. So many joined the ranks of Gethsemani that it was able to establish two daughter houses.

Merton's readers saw that he was a fragile man, a vulnerable man very much like themselves; a man willing, however, to share with others his interior journey. If the world lacked peace, he said, then men must seek it in themselves. Much of Merton's writing echoed Christ's words: "The kingdom of heaven is within" (see Lk 17:21) and showed that the method to reach this center was through contemplation. We should remember that Merton had only recently become aware of the definition of the word *contemplation*. Now, he shared what he had learned about the contemplative life with his readers, an endeavor made more intimate by the very nature of his journalistic style of writing. Merton described this style as "nothing more than a collection of notes and personal reflections." Readers felt comfortable with Merton who promised that the contemplative experience was not something esoteric and available to only a privileged few, but available to all Christians, a message he relayed in vibrant, easy to understand prose devoid of theological jargon.

Similar to Pascal's *Pensees* which inspired him, *Seeds of Contemplation* was a collection of brief, epigrammatic reflections on various aspects of the contemplative life. It was a book not to be read in one sitting, but one to be pondered over a period time in order to allow the "seeds of contemplation" to take root in the reader's soul. Although American readers enthusiastically responded to it, Merton was not pleased with the book, or more accurately, he was ambivalent about it. Once he said he thought that it was too "cold and cerebral," lacking "warmth and human affection." Yet at another time he said it is one of his books that he would stand by even though he admits to making a "stupid" remark about the Sufis.

Today critics are also split about it: Michael Mott sees the book as a masterpiece of spiritual writing; William Shannon sees it as an immature and naive book.[3] The truth is that it is both: it contains passages of beautiful prose along with insightful advice about the spiritual journey, but it is also marred by Merton's *contemptus mundi*.

Soon after its publication, Merton himself realized that *Seeds of Contemplation* contained passages that revealed his graphically obvious shadow projection, passages he eventually toned down when he revised it in the late forties and again in the early sixties when he expanded and renamed it *New Seeds of Contemplation*. One such passage is the following:

> Do everything you can to avoid the amusements and the noise and the business of men. Keep as far away as you can from the places where they gather to cheat and insult one another, to exploit one another, to laugh at one another, or to mock one another with their false gestures of friendship. Do not read their newspapers, if you can help it. Be glad if you can keep beyond the reach of their radios. Do not bother with their unearthly songs or their intolerable concerns for the way their bodies look and feel.[4]

This passage is more lengthy in its denunciation of the world, but this brief excerpt at least illustrates that Merton was very much the man who entered Gethsemani in 1941. The characteristic signs of true spiritual growth are acceptance of and compassion for the world, the kind of compassion shown by Christ who forgave Mary Magdalene, by Christ who forgave those who crucified him. Perhaps compassion for the world outside Gethsemani was impossible to Merton because he had yet to forgive himself for his own past. He had hoped that the stark, austere, harsh life of penance he lived at Gethsemani would transform him into the person he wanted to be, a saint. He had yet to learn to live in the present moment, to accept himself, and to leave saintliness to God. The alienated Merton of Cambridge, of Columbia, who rejected the world in 1941 by leaving it to enter a monastery, was still rejecting the world in 1947-48. So it is not surprising to read further on in *Seeds of Contemplation* Merton's condemnatory metaphor for the world,

> I have very little idea of what is going on in the world: but occasionally I happen to see some of the things they are drawing and writing there and it gives me the conviction that they are all living in *ash cans*. It makes me glad I cannot hear what they are singing.[5]

The very use of such an extremely negative image for the world, "ash can," suggests Merton is trapped by a rather powerful, unconscious emotion; thus, in keeping the world at a distance he also keeps at a distance (buried in the unconscious) his own shadow. The ash can, however, is an apt metaphor for the unconscious. As we throw the refuse of daily life into the ash can, so too do we often relegate things about ourselves into the ash can of the unconscious, especially those negative truths about ourselves that Jung refers to as the shadow. It is poignant today to see the poorest of the poor, the humble homeless, go from ash can to ash can in search of food, in search of items to use in their poor lives. They at least know that much that is good and still usable can be found in ash cans. Jung encourages all people on the inner journey to take a good look into their own psychic ash cans, and not to be repulsed by what they encounter; there is much good there, "gold not dross," which can lead to growth in self-knowledge.

At this stage of his interior journey (late forties), Merton felt safe and secure within Gethsemani's holy walls, even his first impression of Gethsemani as the center of America, holding it together, suffered a sea change. He comments in *Seeds of Contemplation* "there are not twenty men alive in the world now, who see things as they really are." Later he qualifies his comment by saying, "I don't believe that there are twenty men alive in the world. But there must be one or two."[6] We assume that he includes the world of Gethsemani: truly a severe and pessimistic world view.

It is interesting to notice that with *Seeds of Contemplation* Merton sets forth his theory of the false and the true self. He writes: "Every one of us is *shadowed* by an illusory person: a false self." This image of the self, Merton says, is one that "exists only in my own egocentric desires."[7]

The notion of the "false self" is one Merton borrowed from Bernard of Clairveaux. Merton writes:

> After all, what is your personal identity? It is what you really are, your real self. None of us is what he thinks he is, or what other people think he is, still less what his passport says he is. Many of us think, no doubt, that we are what would like to be. And it is fortunate for most of us that we are mistaken. We do

not generally know what is good for us. That is because, in St. Bernard's language, our true personality has been concealed under the "disguise" of a false self, the ego whom we tend to worship in place of God.[8]

This idea corresponds to Jung's belief that in the first stages of individuation the ego considers itself the center of the psyche rather than the Self, the God within. Jung says,

Anyone who has any ego-consciousness at all takes it for granted that he knows himself. But the ego knows only its own contents, not the unconscious and its contents. People measure their self-knowledge by what the average person in their social environment knows of himself, but not by the real psychic facts which are for the most part hidden from them. In this respect the psyche behaves like the body of whose physiological and anatomical structure the average person knows very little too.[9]

The ego constructs a disguise or a persona, to use Jung's term, which obfuscates its relationship to the Self. This mask is also presented to the world; it is not a reflection of the Self, quite the contrary; often it is a flattering mask that pretends to qualities the person does not possess. The more false the persona, the more ego-oriented the individual. People are often fooled by persons who wear well-constructed masks until in a moment of carelessness the mask falls off, revealing the egotism of the wearer. This can be a humiliating moment for the person involved, for he realizes how much of his life is based upon a lie. Or, it can be a freeing moment if one is open to it.

An individuated person, however, understands the true function of the persona: he wears his persona consciously, and he adopts one that is true to his personality type. An individuated person knows he is not the persona. He also understands the social necessity of a persona. It is primarily a means toward protecting one's vulnerability, and at the same time allowing healthy interaction with other people.

In *Seeds of Contemplation* Merton is preoccupied with the idea of false and true self because in the early stages of his career as monk/writer there was a tendency among his readers to canonize the young monk. With the publication of *The Seven Storey Mountain*, Merton received encomia from the likes of Evelyn Waugh, Grahame Greene, and Clare Booth Luce. Fulton Sheen compared his autobiography to Augustine's *Confessions*. Merton could easily have been a victim of a bad case of ego-**inflation**. In fact, Merton may have rightfully felt uneasy about presenting himself to the world as an authority on the spiritual life when in such matters he was himself truly a novice. Perhaps he felt that he was hiding behind a false self, a persona, an attractive one of the humble but wise monk/mystic. We can imagine Merton thinking to himself, "If they only knew the real me." If he had been plagued by such thoughts (not being what he appeared to be) when he applied to the Franciscans, it is likely that he was still plagued by such thoughts at Gethsemani.

It is also likely that Merton himself thought it presumptuous to write an autobiography or to write a book about spirituality: he had been baptized a Catholic when he was twenty-three (1938); he had entered Gethsemani at twenty-seven, had been a monk only three years when he began his autobiography and only six years when he began *Seeds of Contemplation*. There were without a doubt many holy monks at Gethsemani, monks who for decades had struggled through the valleys and had reached the peaks of the contemplative life. What right had Merton to present himself as one of the proficients? So when Merton writes at length about the true and false self, it is aimed very likely at himself as much as at his readers.

This may explain his own ambivalence about *Seeds of Contemplation*. If Merton had been permitted to tell in his autobiography the full truth about his life in England and his fathering of a child, he may not have been so bothered by the notion of false and true self. Such biographical lacunae must have distressed Merton; every time he came across the biblical injunction, "The truth will make you free" (Jn 8:32), he must have winced.

In addition, he was still intent upon a quest to capture that illusive goal of perfection. He writes: "The only true joy on earth is to escape from the prison of our own self-hood.... Short of this perfection, created things do not bring us joy but pain."[10] True joy and peace, Jung says, comes not from escape but from the embrace of opposites, of the dark and the light residing in each one of us. Merton's divided psyche is clearly revealed in the following passage, a prayer illustrating Merton's desire to remain separated from his shadow,

> Therefore keep me, above all things, *from* sin. Keep me *from* the death of deadly sin which puts hell in my soul. Keep me *from* the murder of lust that blinds and poisons my heart. Keep me *from* the sins that eat a man's flesh with irresistible fire until he is devoured.

Keep me *from* loving money in which is hatred, from avarice and ambition that suffocate my life. Keep me *from* the vain works of vanity and the thankless labor in which artists destroy themselves for pride and money and reputation.... Untie my hands and deliver my heart from sloth. Set me free *from* the laziness that goes about disguised as activity when activity is useless, and *from* the cowardice that does what is not demanded in order to escape sacrifice.[11]

If we need a description of Merton's shadow, the above passage suffices. His prayer could be summarized, "Lord, keep me from my shadow," a prayer that leads only to frustration and continuing lack of self-knowledge. But no matter what lengths individuals go to in order to ignore their shadow, it will manifest itself either in projections or dreams. Merton would have been wiser to accept his shadow, realize it, and embrace it. This would have provided the peace and freedom he so longed for. This does not mean to suggest that Merton should have lived out his shadow, rather it should have been transformed into a positive source of energy for the development of his personality. But this cannot be accomplished until a person owns that part of the self.

We do not wish to belabor Merton's ongoing problem with his shadow, for even as he writes *Seeds of Contemplation* he knows in his heart that true sanctity's *sine qua non* is love for all people: "I must look for my identity somehow, not only in God but in other men."[12] The word "somehow" is a poignant *crie de coeur* because Merton intellectually understands he must learn to love the world of men and women, the problem is the means. Merton's very way of living (examination of conscience, prayer, fasting, and silence) would provide the necessary breakthrough. Unlike many people in the world, Merton was fortunate to live in an ambience of quiet and solitude which of its very nature fosters the inward gaze, one reaching into the darkest recesses of the soul.

Such a close scrutiny of oneself, of course, requires courage. Many people are afraid to peer into their souls, to face the truth about themselves. Only when the illusions and falsehoods of the self are stripped away can a person see himself for what he really is, at the same time freeing himself to see the world as it really is. Thus, it will take time (the first half of his monastic life) before Merton is ready to take back his projections. In the first years of his monastic life Merton had yet to understand that psychological projection is really a diversionary tactic employed by the ego to keep an individual from self-knowledge and to keep the shadow in its place of darkness in the unconscious. By the time he writes *Conjectures of a Guilty Bystander* he will have transformed his inward gaze into an outward gaze which compassionately views the world.

But long before the publication of *Conjectures of a Guilty Bystander* we see in the introduction to the second section of his journal *The Sign of Jonas* (early fifties) Merton's first admission that he was a victim of a severe case of psychological projection. He writes: "Perhaps the things I had resented about the world when I left it were defects of my own that I had projected upon it."[13] This is a moment of epiphany in Merton's individuation. Jung himself says that recognition of projections is itself "a moral achievement beyond the ordinary."

After recognition of the shadow, the next stage is to embrace the shadow. Intellectually recognizing that one has a shadow, that one is defective, or rather sinful, is certainly painful. Many Christians find it difficult to forgive themselves. Christ's exhortation to love our neighbors as we love ourselves is not as easy as it sounds. Too many people do not love themselves, are not able to accept their fallibility, and punish themselves in a variety of ways for not being perfect. Consequently, they suffer from a number psychic and psychosomatic problems, from religious scrupulosity, guilt, and self-hatred to physical problems such as ulcers or colitis.

When people achieve an understanding of projection, they achieve insights into their own selves. They often feel as if a great burden has been lifted from their shoulders which is followed by a sense of freedom, one that makes life more enjoyable. They become more whole human beings.

Jungian Jolande Jacobi writes:

> The ego and its antagonist, the shadow, represent an archetypal motif … and indeed experience confirms that the conscious realization of the shadow, the disclosure of its qualities, and the integration of its contents always have a therapeutic effect because this is a step on the way towards man's wholeness.[14]

Merton spent the first nine years of his monastic life in inner turmoil, and it took its toll. After his ordination (1949) he was immobilized by health problems and nervous exhaustion. Perhaps living in the "belly of a paradox" proved too much for him, for like Jonas, he was still driven in two directions: on the one hand he wanted to be a saint but on the other hand he could not escape himself. About such a psychic dilemma Jung says:

It is well to remind ourselves of St. Paul and his split consciousness: on one side he felt he was the apostle directly called and enlightened by God, and on the other hand a sinful man who could not pluck out the "thorn in the flesh" and rid himself of the Satanic angel who plagued him. That is to say, even the most enlightened person remains what he is, and is never more than his own limited ego before the One who dwells within him, whose form has no knowable boundaries, who encompasses him on all sides, fathomless as the abysms of the earth and vast as the sky.[15]

Merton, however, was nearing the end of his purgation, the stripping away of the personae and the taking back of projections. He had cleansed his spiritual "doors of perception" to more fully see his true self. Self-acceptance leads to acceptance of others; therefore, the need to project disappears. And because one has learned to accept, forgive, and love oneself, one is freed to do the same for others. We are reminded of King Lear who, after being stripped of title, kingdom, followers, of everything his ego valued, sees his own foolishness and shifts his gaze for the first time from himself to others:

Poor naked wretches, wheresoe'er you are,
That bide the pelting of this pitiless storm,
How shall your houseless heads and unfed sides,
Your looped and windowed raggedness, defend you
from seasons such as these? O, I have ta'en
Too little care of this! Take physic, pomp;
Expose thyself to feel what wretches feel,
That thou may'st shake the superflux to them
And show the heavens more just.[16]

Stripped of everything the world and his ego valued, Merton too could cry "O, I have ta'en too little care of this!"—that is, the suffering of mankind. Such an insight would come, but not until he faced, accepted, and integrated his shadow; and then he would have to face, accept, and integrate his anima, "the masterpiece of individuation," to be addressed in upcoming chapters.

FIVE

THE JOURNEY TO WHOLENESS

> The heat is upon us but it is not too bad. We are starting a new routine of night watches around here—to guard against fires. We take turns going around the house for two hours while everyone else is asleep. I am on tonight and think it is quite probably going to be fun.[1]

Thus begins Merton's fire watch duty immortalized in the Epilogue to *The Sign of Jonas*, "Fire Watch, July 4, 1952" which many people consider to be Merton's finest prose work. Jacques Maritain extolled it as the most beautiful spiritual writing composed in the twentieth century.[2] It is a prose poem of haunting, shimmering beauty, graceful rhythm, and rich symbolism. And as with great prose and poetry, it offers to its readers a wealth of associations, resonances, and interpretations.

"Fire Watch" symbolizes Merton's merging of both vocations, that of writer and contemplative, in language that transcends duality and reaches toward the ineffable beauty of God. It also serves as a summary of the first phase of Merton's individuation (prior to and up to July 4, 1952) involving the integration of the various facets of his personality whose ultimate goal was psychic and spiritual wholeness.

The Sign of Jonas reveals Merton's intimate identification with that biblical figure whose experience Jung describes as the archetypal "night sea journey."[3] Thus a Jungian analysis of Merton's "Fire Watch" not only illuminates more fully Merton's inner journey but also emphasizes more clearly its universality, rendering it relevant to believers and unbelievers alike.

It may be useful to review the archetypal myth of Jonas. Jonas is summoned by God to journey to Nineveh to preach repentance to its inhabitants. Instead, Jonas disobeys God's command by sailing in the opposite direction to Tharsis. While he is at sea (in more ways than one), a great storm arises, buffeting and endangering the ship with its men and cargo. The frightened mariners, hoping to salvage the ship and themselves, jettison small wares to lighten the vessel. Meanwhile, as the storm rages, Jonas retires to the inner section of the ship to sleep. Later, with no abatement of the tempest, Jonas awakes and admits that he is the sole cause of the storm, having disobeyed the will of God.

To save the ship and its men, Jonas willingly offers to sacrifice his life, allowing the mariners to cast him into the tumultuous sea. Immediately a great fish swallows him, and for three days he remains captive in the dark belly of the fish which transports him into the deepest caverns of the ocean. Then, as a result of his praying to God, Jonas is vomited onto dry land where he resumes his journey—not to Tharsis, but to Nineveh.

While at Nineveh, Jonas so successfully preaches repentance to the people that all the inhabitants clothe themselves in sackcloth and ashes in reparation for their sins. God is moved to pity and mercifully spares them and their city. However, Jonas, feeling he has been deceived, is angered by God's turnabout. He seethes in self-pity until one day, in a moment of selflessness, he expresses compassion for a dying plant. At this instant God reveals to Jonas his reason for sparing Nineveh: if mere man is able to pity a sick creature he did not create, cannot God be merciful to his own children?

Jonas' archetypal sea journey serves effectively as a paradigm of Jung's theory of individuation. All people are called to wholeness (God's summons to Jonas). The call may come at any stage of life, but it is strongest at mid-life. The call may be either ignored or obeyed. Too often we do not heed the summons, often deliberately escaping wholeness by evasion (Jonas' traveling to Tharsis). However, the penalty for not heeding the unconscious (the *locus Dei*) is severe, resulting in psychological and spiritual turmoil (the storm) which can seriously upset our lives to the point that we try to escape our real and immediate problems (Jonas asleep), or we solve them superficially (jettisoning light wares). But courage must be mustered to confront the deep psyche where true self-knowledge resides (Jonas thrown into the sea). The embarkation into the unconscious to face those unknown aspects of ourselves, or aspects slightly known but unacknowledged and feared, cannot be a direct confrontation. Direct confrontation risks annihilation. Thus the need for an intermediary, Jonas' fish. And a journey willingly and knowingly accepted will eventually result in rebirth (Jonas' return to land). Rebirth, as the word implies, is just the beginning; individuation is a lifetime process. Jonas still has much to experience, to learn. As with the Ancient Mariner whose albatross was unfettered from his neck only after he blessed God's creatures of the sea (acceptance of unconscious elements), so too with Jonas: his enlightenment, initiated in the sea, leads him to compassion for a helpless, dying plant; thus, the once "dying" Jonas is led to a more whole/holy life by accepting and fulfilling his destiny which is the will of God.

This paradigm of Jung's theory of individuation can be applied to Merton's "Fire Watch, July 4, 1952." The July 4 date is significant. It celebrates the birth of the United States and Merton's recent American citizenship recorded in section six of his published journal. The date also symbolizes the continual birth and rebirth that is Merton's interior life, all of which is integral to his journey to wholeness, his journey to God.

The superficial, and also serious, purpose of the night round is to detect fire in the monastery. On a deeper level the journey is a search for the fire of purgation and illumination. At the halfway point of the fire watch (mid-life), Merton recognizes this critical and profound aspect of his journey when he concludes that his monastic vocation is God's way of isolating him "to search your soul with lamps and questions" (Jonas isolated in the belly of the fish). The fire watch becomes what Merton designates an "examination of conscience," or as Jung would describe it, a "circumambulation of the self" whose purpose is self-knowledge which leads to wholeness, or, if you will, holiness. Jung remarks, "Self-knowledge, in the form of an examination of conscience, is demanded by Christian ethics. They were very pious people who maintained that self-knowledge paves the way to knowledge of God."[4] The round journey through the quadrangular, cloistered monastery traces a mandala: a circle within a square which is the symbol of wholeness, for Jung views quaternity as the symbol par excellence of the integrated psyche.[5]

Helpful to our understanding of "Fire Watch" as a symbolic journey is to bear in mind that Merton's buffer against total engulfment by darkness (the unconscious) is the monastery itself. The monastery is Merton's "fish," or, as he describes it, his "holy monster." The monastery aids Merton in delving into the deepest aspects of his psyche where he will confront many things about himself, about Gethsemani, and about the human family.

Before the fire watch begins, Merton decks himself not with weapons, as heroic figures of the past did preparing for war, but with ordinary, symbolic tools: flashlight, sneakers, keys, and a clock. Merton is a modern hero—a watchman of the inner life. Each of these tools has its obvious function for the fire watch, but each also symbolizes various aspects of the archetypal journey to wholeness. The flashlight represents the eye of consciousness (ego) capable of rendering attention to the darkest areas of the psyche. The sneakers, reminiscent of the sandals of fleet-footed Mercury who led souls into the underworld, remind us that the individuation process requires silence, the *sine qua non* of the inner life, for only in silence can one hear the still, small voice of the Self. The keys represent the insights, dreams, surmises, and memories that will open the darkest and deepest rooms of the psyche, yielding gem-like truths about ourselves, especially the truth about our shadow which Jung defines as "the thing a person has no wish to be."[6] The clock is a constant reminder that we live in time and therefore we must lose no time in realizing the Self. Individuation is urgent business.

Merton, who elsewhere describes himself as a "solitary explorer" dedicated to investigating areas of the psyche "deeper than the bottom of anxiety," commences his journey in the lowest section of the monastery, the cellar, where he walks not on concrete but on Mother Earth. Here he meets with "naked wires, stinks of the hides of slaughtered calves," all representative of the instinctual facets of a man's life, of the particular aspects of Merton's personality which had to be faced, accepted, and integrated into his life as a monk.

At the end of a long catacomb in the cellar, Merton encounters a "brand-new locked door into the guest wing that was only finished the other day." This door is not to be opened. The guest wing symbolizes the world which Merton is not ready to face. At that time in his life he was still embarked on an inner journey which would eventually lead him outward to the world in love and compassion. This would emerge in his next major journal *Conjectures of a Guilty Bystander*. Both Jung and Merton write that the journey to wholeness necessitates love for others. Jung writes, "Individuation does not shut one out from the world, but gathers the world to oneself."[7] From the number of people who visited Merton at Gethsemani and from the scope of his letter writing, we know that Merton, indeed, gathered the world to himself. Merton writes, "A man cannot enter into the deepest center of himself and pass through that center into God, unless he is able to pass entirely out of himself and give to other people in the purity of selfless love."[8] But for Merton on the fire-watch, the time was not ripe; he was not ready for the world.

On his way to the bakery, the second station of the night round, a pattern reminiscent of Christ's stations of the cross, Merton encounters the monastery's old furnace where he was ordered to burn Abbot Frederick's letters. We think of the "old" Merton of London, New York, Columbia, who through the spiritual fire of purgation and monastic forging, becomes the new Merton, Father Louis of Gethsemani. We also recall Merton's similar break with his own past when, before entering Gethsemani, he burned his papers except for one journal, one novel, and the best of his poetry. In this fire of individuation Merton continues to burn away the false selves, the deception, the falsehood, all that would interfere with his attainment of his true Self which is Christ.

Walking farther on in the cellar near the bakery, now with his feet on concrete, Merton glimpses jars of various kinds of fruits: the bakery and the fruits both suggest that, if needed, the unconscious always yields nourishment for the **libido** (energy) necessary to continue the journey to self-knowledge. Interestingly and appropriately, at this point along the dark journey, Merton's flashlight illuminates an engraving of the Holy Face, a reminder of two important facts: Christ is the goal of the inner journey, and knowledge of Christ leads one to an awareness of the truth about one's life.

As he rounds the corner to the next station, the novitiate, Merton comes face to face with his monastic past and with the mystery of his vocation. This difficult and painful stage of individuation requires complete honesty and humility in recognizing and accepting the past along with its deceits, its errors, its sins, all of which, in general, Jung describes as the shadow. Merton finds his past to be almost unreal, he barely recognizes his former self. But in scrutinizing his past, he realizes: "The things I thought important ... have turned out to be of small value. And the things that I never thought about ... were the things that mattered."[9]

Only a mature person, very much conscious of his inner journey, could make such an admission. About this kind of individuation Jung writes:

> The difference between the "natural" individuation process, which runs its course unconsciously, and the one which is consciously realized, is tremendous. In the first case consciousness nowhere intervenes; the end remains as dark as the beginning. In the second case so much darkness comes to light that the personality is permeated with light, and consciousness necessarily gains in scope and insight. The encounter between conscious and unconscious has to ensure that the light which shines in the darkness is not only comprehended by the darkness, but comprehends it.[10]

Merton then enters into the first of his lovely, lyrical addresses to God: "God, my God Whom I meet in darkness...." We hear a person comfortable and unafraid to engage his God, to express his doubts, his fears, and his hopes. Such an encounter is characteristic of conscious individuation because the conscious ego creates an axis with the Self, a state of being which leads to further enlightenment, further wholeness.

Merton returns to the little cloister, a reminder of his scholastics, "souls entrusted to me." Here we observe

Merton, appointed to the position of master of scholastics, moving outward to others in care and compassion. This shift of gaze from the I to others is a natural and inevitable movement of the inner journey. He then advances to the door of the ceramic studio beyond which lie the burned out kiln and the newly purchased kiln. As the furnace suggests purgation, the kiln suggests strengthening. Again we recall Merton before his entry into Gethsemani, a man disillusioned and "burned out" by the values of the modern world; and Merton the monk, a man strengthened in his acceptance of his humanity and that of others, a man who tenderly recalls his young scholastic who "suddenly made a good crucifix." About this young scholastic and his other scholastics he is anxious:

> I think of this simple and mysterious child, and of all my other scholastics. What is waiting to be born in all their hearts? Suffering? Deception? Heroism? Defeat? Peace? Betrayal? Sanctity? Death? Glory?

Obviously, Merton is aware of the possible costs and rewards of the inner journey. Elsewhere he writes that the inner journey is an "anguished and sometimes perilous exploration." Jung also warns us about the cost of individuation:

> Everything good is costly, and the development of personality is one of the most costly of all things. It is a matter of saying yea to oneself, of taking oneself as the most serious of tasks, of being conscious of everything one does, and keeping it constantly before one's eyes in all its dubious aspects—truly a task that taxes us to the utmost. [11]

At this juncture of the journey Merton recapitulates: he is amazed to have encountered such "strange caverns in the monastery's history, layers set down by years of geographical strata: you feel like an archaeologist unearthing ancient civilizations."

Merton's description of the substrata of the monastery parallels in astounding similarity Jung's dream in which Jung found himself exploring the basement of his home that led to a subcellar under which he discovered a cavern, all of which served for Jung as a model of the human psyche that ultimately led him to his theory of the collective unconscious. About his dream Jung commented:

> It obviously pointed to the foundation of cultural history—a history of successive layers of consciousness. My dream thus constituted a kind of structural diagram of the human psyche.[12]

In addition to this remarkable coincidence is the fact that both Merton and Jung refer to themselves as archaeologists, not of past civilizations, but of the human psyche.

Thus far Merton's journey has rendered him aware of the history of the monastery, his own personal history, the history of the human race, all intertwined into one history. He also admits that the monastery has changed much since his entry ten years ago: "Ten years have as many meanings as ten Egyptian dynasties." Merton, too, has dramatically changed, yet he must continue to explore these meanings which apply not only to Gethsemani but also to himself, since individuation is an ongoing process that ends only in death.

He now comes to the church. Here Merton learned to pray; here he took his vows; here he was ordained priest; and here he celebrated the holy mystery of the Mass every day of his life. The church serves as the belly of Merton's holy monster, the monastery. It is a place of purification, assimilation, nourishment, and a place of passage—for Merton must pass through the church before he can reach the tower, and through the tower, God. "Now is the time to get up and go to the tower. Now is the time to meet you, God." Towers are often viewed as symbolic of our yearning for the infinite, for God. For Jung towers are mandalas, symbols of the integrated Self. But Merton realizes he is not ready for the climb to the tower; he still must make rounds of the second and third floors of the monastery.

Continuing the fire watch, Merton arrives at the library, the abode of collective wisdom, again bringing to mind Jung's collective unconscious along with its archetypes. He must also pass through the third room of the library, the one named "hell," the storage room of condemned books, suggesting Jung's concept of the shadow, all that would be kept from the daylight of consciousness. He then proceeds to the upper scriptorium. Consider Merton's propensity for speaking honestly about his life in a number of genres: autobiography, journals, letters, essays, and poetry.

On his way to the third floor, Merton walks softly through the dormitory, "perhaps the longest room in Kentucky." Here much is "shrouded in shadows." This room where all the monks of Gethsemani sleep suggests that much of the psyche remains in the dark of unconsciousness. Sleep, however, offers dreams, the primary key to the unconscious. Understanding the importance of dreams as a means of deeper self-knowledge, Merton recorded many of them in his journals.

Jung encourages everyone to remember, to record, and to analyze dreams:

> The dream is a little door in the innermost secret recesses of the soul, opening that cosmic night which was psyche long before there was any ego-consciousness, and which will remain psyche no matter how far our ego-consciousness extends.[13]

The fire watch journey now takes Merton to "a door hidden between two cells"—reminiscent of Dante's secret exit from the Inferno. He enters the annex leading to the infirmary and its chapel where Merton made retreats before the important rites of passage in his life as a monk: clothing, professions, and ordination. The infirmary is the locus of regained health, of wholeness. At one point of the journey, Merton remarks that the monastery is "like a sick person who has recovered."

In reality it is Merton who has recovered. The time is ripe; Merton is ready to climb the tower: "Now the business is done. Now I shall ascend to the top of this religious city, leaving its modern history behind."

Unlocking the padlock of the door to the tower "always makes a great noise." Now Merton begins his climb up the stairs, a perilous climb: "You have to watch the third step or your feet go through the boards." The inner journey is fraught with danger: one must always be as conscious as possible of what one is doing. When Merton finally reaches the top, he opens the door which "swings open upon a vast sea of darkness and of prayer." And what follows is a poetic description of the surrounding valley with its moonlight, stars, hills, and great chorus of sounds.

Merton then prepares himself to address his God by placing the clock on the belfry ledge and by sitting cross-legged against the tower. The clock is no longer needed, for Merton has gone beyond time. He has arrived at the still center of the tower where heaven and earth and time and eternity intersect. His prayer commences with a litany of questions directed to God even though Merton recognizes that "there is a greater comfort in the substance of silence than in the answer to a question." Subsequently, he realizes that it is God who initiates dialogue, as he always has. It is God who utters Merton's name, and it is Merton who listens to what he always knew: "The voice of God is heard in paradise."

Then follows Merton's loveliest language, reserved for the voice of God, eloquently expressing the paradoxical nature of the inner journey that both contains and is contained by the love, mercy, and infinity of God, the "I am" of every inner journey of every person:

> What was poor has become infinite. What is now merciful was never cruel. I have always overshadowed Jonas with My mercy, and cruelty I know not at all. Have you had sight of Me, Jonas My child? Mercy within mercy within mercy. I have forgiven the universe without end, because I have never known sin.

Perhaps the key to a Jungian understanding of Merton's journey is found in this one sentence of the epilogue: "The night contains values the day never dreamed of." With the night symbolic of the unconscious mind and the day symbolic of the conscious mind, Merton's insight summarizes succinctly and ex-

actly Jung's own findings about the psyche: the individual psyche is a combination of light and shadow,
of consciousness and unconsciousness, including what
Jung describes as the collective unconscious, the
repository of humanity's psychic heritage, the abode of
the archetypes. The nocturnal fire watch duty leads
Merton to the realization that to plunge into the night
(the unconscious) is to embark on a journey to self-
realization, to wholeness. And to both Merton and Jung
there is not a more important journey than this inner
one.

PART TWO

MERTON'S ENCOUNTER WITH HIS ANIMA

SIX

PROVERB:
MERTON'S ANIMA

The anima is personified in dreams by images of women ranging from seductress to spiritual guide. It is associated with the eros principle, hence a man's anima development is reflected in how he relates to women. Within his own psyche, his anima functions as his soul, influencing his ideas, attitudes and emotions.[1]

An analysis from a Jungian perspective of Thomas Merton's dreams reveals that his encounter with his anima resulted in two remarkable events: the epiphany of the Louisville Vision and the creation of the fascinating prose poem *Hagia Sophia*.

Jung believed everyone is psychologically androgynous. He designates a man's feminine component the anima and a woman's masculine component the animus. Psychological growth for both a man and a woman demands the assistance of the contrasexual archetype. The specific function of a man's anima is to serve as a mediatrix between the ego, the center of the conscious mind, and the Self, the center of the unconscious mind and the regulating force of the whole psyche. When a man listens to his anima, he is led into the deepest regions of the unconscious mind where the sources of wisdom and self-knowledge lie. The anima also assists a man in discovering the personal symbols which will release Eros, the principle of relatedness without which he cannot connect with the Self or with people in the external world. The anima likewise provides the libido (energy) necessary for the further development of the personality. Jungian analyst John Sanford writes:

> When the anima functions in her correct place, she serves to broaden and enlarge a man's consciousness, and to enrich his personality by infusing into him, through dreams, fantasies, and inspired ideas, an awareness of an inner world of psychic images and life-giving emotions. A man's consciousness tends to be too constricted, and without contact with the unconscious, becomes dry and sterile.[2]

Since it is in dreams that the anima most often appears, interpretation of dreams is the cornerstone of Jung's psychology and analytic method. Jung recorded and interpreted many of his dreams in his autobiography *Memories, Dreams, Reflections*. He viewed dreams as "utterances of the unconscious," and the primary means through which the unconscious communicates with the conscious mind. Dreams, therefore, are symbolic letters that, if decoded wisely, reveal much about one's personality. In his own encounter with his anima, Jung records the following:

> Then a new idea came to me: in putting down all this material for analysis I was in effect writing letters to the anima, that is, to a part of myself with a different viewpoint from my conscious one.[3]

He later says about the anima:

It is she who communicates the images of the unconscious to the conscious mind, and that is what I
chiefly valued her for. For decades I always turned to
the anima when I felt that my emotional behavior
was disturbed....[4]

Merton, too, recorded many of his dreams in his
published and unpublished journals. Obviously he
believed that they were an important part of his inner
life and that an understanding of his dreams would lead
to increased self-knowledge. Many of his dreams, like
the following one recorded on February 28, 1958, con-
cern the anima:

On a porch at Douglaston I am embraced with determined and virginal passion by a young Jewish girl.
She clings to me and will not let me go, and I get to
like the idea. I see that she is a nice kid in a plain,
sincere sort of way. I reflect, "She belongs to the same
race as St. Anne." I ask her name and she says her
name is Proverb. I tell her that is a beautiful and
significant name, but she does not appear to like
it—perhaps others have mocked her for it.[5]

The dream ego, Merton at his current age, and the
Jewish girl, much younger, the Eternal Feminine, meet
on the porch of his grandparents' home. The porch,
symbol of receptivity (at one time in American life the
traditional locus of girl-boy encounters), is really a
threshold or an entrance to the rest of the house. The
house symbolizes the psyche. The girl is Merton's
anima. When she embraces him with "virginal passion"
they are unified, one man/woman. Thus, the embrace
is symbolic of *coniunctio* which Jung defines as the
inner marriage. Being a man and true to the logos
impulse in all men, Merton asks her name. She gives a

symbolic name, "Proverb." A proverb is a wise saying; hence, Proverb is a spiritual guide, a wise woman who will lead Merton into the house of the psyche where he too will attain true wisdom. Merton deduces that Proverb is "mocked by others." These others are elements of Merton's own personality which disparage holy wisdom or the feminine in general in favor of the rational, intellectual, masculine way of the world. The Jews, the stewards of holy wisdom from time immemorial, have often been mocked. They are "the same race as St. Anne," the mother of Mary, the mother of God.

A close reading of this dream also suggests some noteworthy biographical information about Merton. Merton's father and mother were married in St. Anne's Church in Soho, London. He named his first hermitage, an old abandoned tool shed at Gethsemani, after St. Anne. And as a young man attending school in England, Merton met his friend Andrew Winsor's sister Ann. She made such a lasting impression on him that in 1965, over thirty years after their meeting, Merton wrote:

> The other day after Mass I suddenly thought of Ann Winsor, Andrew's little sister. She was about twelve or thirteen when I used to visit at his parent's parsonage on the Isle of Wight. I remember that quiet rectory in the shady valley of Brooke. She was the quietest thing in it. A dark and secret child. One does not fall in love with a child of thirteen and I hardly remember even thinking of her or noticing her, yet the other day I realized that I had never forgotten her and that she had made a deep impression. [6]

Consider also that, when Merton lived with his grandparents in Douglaston, he often used the porch as a place to read:

> The first two months after I landed in New York, and went to the house in Douglaston, I continued to read the Bible surreptitiously—I was afraid someone might make fun of me. And since I slept on the sleeping porch, which opened on the upstairs hall through glass doors and which, in any case, I shared with my uncle, I no longer dared to pray on my knee. ... [7]

That sleep would be associated with the Douglaston porch, along with reading the Bible (perhaps the Book of Proverbs) and Merton's sense of shame ("others have mocked her for it") in reading the Bible, adds to our appreciation of this dream, a dream resonating with hints about Merton's life and personality.

To enter more deeply into the significance of his dream, Merton initiates a dialogue with Proverb through a series of love letters. Jung would laud this active engagement of his anima since it is a form of **active imagination**, a method of communing with unconscious elements in order to elicit their full import. In these letters, Merton thanks Proverb for appearing to him in his dreams and for awakening in him things that he thought he had lost forever.

In a letter to Proverb dated March 4, 1958 Merton noted the great difference in their ages and wrote:

> How grateful I am to you for loving in me something which I thought I had entirely lost, and someone who, I thought, had long ago ceased to be.... Dearest Proverb, I love your name, its mystery, its simplicity

and its secret, which even you yourself seem not to appreciate.[8]

Merton's description of his anima along with its nomenclature correlates in remarkable similarity with Jung's own diction about anima:

> Something strangely meaningful clings to her ... a secret knowledge or hidden wisdom ... in her lies something like a hidden purpose which seems to reflect a superior knowledge of life's laws.[9]

What exactly did Merton think he had lost? Perhaps the severity of his mother who wrote him a letter to inform him of her impending death frightened him to the point that he could never completely trust a woman again. He himself writes that "perhaps solitaries are made by severe mothers."[10] Perhaps in his flight from the world and its perceived evils into Gethsemani, Merton became too self-absorbed, too much focused on his own inner journey that he failed to be concerned sufficiently about his brothers and sisters struggling to save their souls in the labyrinthine ways of the world. We recall the young Merton, socially conscious, who volunteered his services to Friendship House in Harlem.

Perhaps Merton just realized that in encountering Proverb he owed much to the women he knew; there were many who enriched his life, women like his grandmother, Aunt Maud, Catherine de Hueck Doherty, Ginny Burton, Naomi Burton Stone, and many others. And now at the age of fifty-three he is writing letters to his own inner woman. The embrace of the anima in this dream is, then, the beginning of a breakthrough in Merton's individuation: it symbolically portrays Merton's willingness to accept the feminine, an acceptance which Jung calls the "masterpiece"[11] of the individuation process. Keep in mind, however, that anima *initiates* the embrace of Merton; she is "determined" and she "clings" to Merton: she is demanding recognition because as her youth suggests, she is the undeveloped aspect of Merton's personality.

On March 18, 1958, Merton experienced his famous Louisville Vision. The following is the original account, not the one revised and included in Merton's journal *Conjectures of a Guilty Bystander*:

> Yesterday, in Louisville, at the corner of 4th and Walnut, suddenly I realized that I loved all the people and that none of them were, or could be, totally alien to me. As if waking from a dream—the dream of my separateness, of my "special" vocation to be different. My vocation does not really make me different from the rest of men or just one in a special category, except artificially, juridically. I am still a member of the human race—and what more glorious destiny is there for man, since the Word was made flesh and became, too, a member of the human race.[12]

This is not the Merton who entered Gethsemani in *contemptus mundi* on December 10, 1941. Nor is this the Merton who eleven years later in the Cincinnati airport thought that the passersby were "infected with some moral corruption that had been brought in by the planes from New York."[13] His embrace, now, of the "human race" is certainly the result of Merton's embrace of the feminine components of his own personality symbolized in his Proverb dream. As a man is physically born of woman, so is man spiritually/psychologically reborn through/by the anima.

The Louisville Vision clearly proves that Merton is moving away from being the "petulant ascetic" of his early years as a monk toward becoming the "radical humanist"[14] of the last decade of his life. Thus, the dogmatic, moralistic, world-denying man of *The Seven Storey Mountain* is the antithesis of the Merton who emerges as the world-embracing monk of the sixties. Consequently, we cannot underestimate the significance of the Louisville Vision, an epiphany which causes Merton to shift his gaze from the narrow, tunnel vision of a Catholic convert to a sweeping, truly catholic gaze that takes in the whole world, its people, and their woe. A scrutiny of Merton's writing after the Louisville Vision clearly illustrates a prolific creativity, his poetic output alone triples, and his new found, broad inclusiveness finds its expression in a myriad of essays on war, peace, nonviolence, racism, cold war, arms control, and Eastern mysticism. Merton writes:

> To choose the world is to choose to do the work I am capable of doing, in collaboration with my brother, to make the world better, more free, more just, more livable, more human.[15]

On March 19, 1958, in his unpublished journal, after a lengthy entry about his Louisville Vision, Merton writes: "It is not a question of proving to myself that I dislike or like the women one sees in the street."[16] No, the issue is much more complex. If we accept Jung's theory that dreams are compensatory mechanisms attempting to rectify an imbalance in the psyche, then Merton's embrace of Proverb points to a failure to embrace the feminine in his own conscious life. That this could happen to a monk who lives, prays, and works in a world of men is not difficult to understand.

Mott indicates that Merton recorded in his journals more about Proverb, her secret beauty and how he "was married to what is most true in all women in the world."[17] Referring to the Louisville Vision in his final letter to Proverb, he writes on the following day:

> I have kept one promise and I have refrained from speaking of you until seeing you again. I knew that when I saw you again it would be very different, in a different place, in a different form, in the most unexpected circumstances. I shall never forget our meeting yesterday. The touch of your hand makes me a different person. To be with you is rest and Truth. Only with you are these things found, dear child, sent to me by God.[18]

Then Mott says, "The letters—and the dreams of Proverb—stopped or were not recorded."[19]

Merton's struggles to love himself and others are far from over, but he at least is more conscious of his problem. On March 30, 1958 Father John of the Cross delivered a Palm Sunday sermon that very much moved Merton. He writes in his journal:

> One reason I am so grateful for this morning's sermon is that my worst and inmost sickness is the despair of ever being able truly to love, because I despair of ever being worthy of love. But the way out is to be able to trust one's friends and thus accept in them acts and things which a sick mind grabs as evidence of lack of love—as pretexts for evading the obligation of love.[20]

Shortly after his Proverb dream sequence, on Tuesday, April 21, 1958, Merton visited the home of his friend

Victor Hammer in nearby Lexington, Kentucky. Hammer was a painter of spiritual themes as well as a publisher of rare, artistic editions of religious books. Delightedly viewing one painting after another, Merton came to an abrupt halt before Hammer's unfinished triptych depicting a young woman offering a crown to a young man. Merton became emotional. He questioned Hammer about the identity of the woman (just as he questioned Proverb). Hammer was uncertain; he explained that the male figure was Christ, but he was unsure about the identity of the woman who could be Mary or some other woman. Mystified, Merton kept returning to the panel to peruse the features of the young maiden.[21]

Why Merton's emotional response? It is likely that Merton unconsciously recognized in the painting his own encounter with his anima. On an unconscious level Merton was grappling with the whole concept of the feminine and its importance in his life. Rather than trying to identify the woman in the painting, Merton would have been better advised to enter its symbolic meaning. The young woman (anima) offers a crown (a symbol of the mandala or wholeness) to a young man. Through the anima comes wholeness, just as through Mary comes all grace. The young man is every man who, when he accepts wholeness, takes upon himself Christ.

Not too long after his experience at the Hammers' home, Merton wrote to Mr. Hammer:

> The feminine principle in the universe is the inexhaustible source of creative realization of the Father's glory in the world and is in fact the manifestation of His glory....[22]

This letter is the origin of the poem *Hagia Sophia*.

Merton arranges his prose poem, *Hagia Sophia*,[23] in the form of a quaternity which follows the canonical hours of lauds, prime, terce, and compline. For Jung quaternity is the symbol of wholeness. Since the poem concerns spiritual/psychic awakening, the poet devotes the first three sections of the poem to the new, morning light: during the hours of lauds (5:30 a.m.), prime (6:00 a.m.), and terce (9:00 a.m.). The last section of the poem occurs at sunset, the hour of compline, the time of completion of the day's work and the singing of the Salve Regina.

In the first section, "Dawn, the Hour of Lauds," Merton, in the voice of the first person singular, compares himself to a man who has just awakened from sleep:

> I am awakened, I am born again at the voice of this my Sister, sent to me from the depths of the divine fecundity.

The Sister (from now on referred to as Anima) is Merton's anima who "rises" from the depths of the unconscious, "the divine fecundity," the locus of the archetypes. Anima brings to Merton a "hidden wholeness" whose origin lies even deeper in the psyche: in "the unseen roots of all created being"—the **collective unconscious**. Note that Anima, like Proverb, is the initiator of the encounter between her and Merton: Merton is "awakened."

Later in this section, Merton compares himself to a man in a hospital, and Anima is likened to a nurse who has "the touch of all life, the touch of the spirit." As a nurse ministers to a sick body, Anima bestows wholeness of spirit upon Merton. However, Anima did not always appear to Merton. There was a time when he "defended himself, fought himself, guarded himself and loved himself alone," a time of egoism and perhaps a reference to his exploitation of women in his youth. And Merton warns the reader that Anima will only come to a man when he is "little" and "helpless" and "poor" and "without defense": he must be a humble man, a man stripped of all masks, a man who knows he is not self-sufficient. Then the poet declares: "This is what it means to recognize Hagia Sophia." Hagia Sophia is Anima. Anima is Holy Wisdom who invites Merton and all men "with unutterable sweetness to be awake and to live."

In the second section, "Early Morning, the Hour of Prime," Merton praises his Anima:

O blessed, silent one, who speaks everywhere!

Although the anima speaks to every man, she can only be heard in silence. However, man refuses to be silent, to listen. In the first person plural, Merton identifies with all men who fail to listen to the anima:

We do not hear the soft voice, the gentle voice, the merciful and feminine.

"We do not hear," is the sad refrain of this section. Merton again warns us that if we do not listen to the anima, we will be denied her fruits: "mercy," "yielding love," "nonresistance," "nonreprisal," and "simplicity." Yet there are some men who listen to their anima, perhaps only one man in a hundred thousand. He is the man who as a result of listening to the inner feminine "has come out of the confused primordial dark night into consciousness." He is the individuated man who has survived the dark night of the soul because he "has expressed the clear silence of Sophia in his own heart." Merton also states that every man's individuation is of infinite importance: "the heavenly lights rejoice in the going forth of one man to make a new world in the morning."

In the next section, "High Morning, the Hour of Terce," Merton evokes the spirit of the fourteenth century:

> When the recluses of the fourteenth century England heard their Church bells and looked out upon the wolds and fens under a kind sky, they spoke in their hearts to "Jesus our Mother." It was Sophia that awakened in their childlike ears.

Clearly, Merton is referring to Lady Julian of Norwich who lovingly invokes Jesus as our mother in her *Revelations of Divine Love*. Merton commenced his poem in the first person singular, then moved on to the inclusive first person plural, and now he joins his voice with the mystic of the fourteenth century who possessed the wisdom early to recognize and accept the feminine in God. And at one point in the poem Merton boldly announces to the reader:

> All the perfections of created things are also in God;
> and therefore He is at once Father and Mother.

The motherhood of God was a daring concept in the fourteenth century, and it remains one in our century. But for Merton to be attracted to this feminine image of God indicates that he is, indeed, coming to terms with his own negative experience of motherhood, ("perhaps solitaries are made by severe mothers"). Merton's attraction to the loving, compassionate Lady Julian is a far cry from the monk who early in his religious life was enamored of the severe, ascetic mystic, St. John of the Cross.

Lady Julian's message is love, that God loves us "not with blame but with pity." To Julian God promised, "All manner of things shall be well." Merton says of Julian:

> Julian is without doubt one of the most wonderful of all Christian voices. She gets greater and greater in my eyes as I grow older and whereas in the old days I used to be crazy about St. John of the Cross, I would not exchange him now for Julian if you gave me the world and the Indies and all the Spanish mystics rolled up in one bundle....[24]

Much of the remainder of this section of the poem concerns Merton's attempt to define Sophia. He is always the man of intellect. He uses her name more than ten times, employing more than ten descriptions of her:

> Hagia Sophia considered as a spontaneous
> participation,
> Sophia is God's sharing of Himself with creatures,
> She is in all things,
> She is union between them,
> She is the love that unites them,
> She is life as communion,
> She is the Bride and the Feast and the Wedding.

Finally, Merton settles for an all-embracing definition of Hagia Sophia, of Anima, by recalling his words set down in a letter to his friend Victor Hammer soon after he viewed Hammer's triptych:

> The feminine principle in the world is the inexhaustible source of creative realizations of the Father's glory. She is His manifestation in radiant

> splendor! But she remains unseen, glimpsed only by
> a few. Sometimes there are none who know her at all.

Merton has amplified his original definition.

The last section, "Sunset, the Hour of Compline, Salve Regina" is the most hauntingly beautiful portion of the poem. We have arrived at the end of the monastic day when all Cistercian monks assemble in the church for the final singing of psalms and the hymn "Salve Regina." According to custom, the church is in darkness, symbolizing the earth's approaching darkness (sunset).

First, Merton meditates on the Virgin Mary, our mother, who is the real "personal manifestation of Sophia." He then says that Mary is "perfect Creature" and "perfectly Redeemed" and "the perfect expression of wisdom in mercy." And it is through Mary that "God enters into His creation." She is our Mother of mercy and our most gracious Advocate.

Then Merton recalls his encounter with the mysterious young maiden of Victor Hammer's triptych:

> She crowns Him not with what is glorious, but with
> what is greater than glory: the one thing greater than
> glory is weakness, nothingness, poverty.

When he first viewed the triptych, he was perplexed about her identity. She was the unknown. But Merton has moved through her mystery into an acceptance of her reality in his life and the life of the Church. She is Sister, she is Anima, she is Hagia Sophia. She sent Christ "to die for us on the cross." She offers a crown of wholeness to every man because Christ accepted the crown of thorns, the Christ who still Himself is "a homeless God, lost in the night, without papers, without identification." But as Sophia is heard, He is heard in silence, in stillness, in darkness.

The Louisville Vision, a moment of epiphany, and *Hagia Sophia*, a poem of immense beauty, both are the fruit of Merton's dream embrace of the mysterious, secret Proverb, his anima.

SEVEN

DREAMS: HIDDEN DOOR TO THE PSYCHE

The dream is a little hidden door in the innermost and most secret recesses of the soul, opening into that cosmic night which was psyche long before there was any ego-consciousness, and which will remain psyche no matter how far our ego-consciousness extends.[1]

As seen in the previous chapter, integration of the anima into consciousness is a vitally important aspect of the individuation process. And although Merton's "Proverb dreams" represent an important breakthrough in Merton's individuation, his integration of the feminine in his psychic life was far from complete. Merton continued to be visited in his dreams by anima figures as shown in his posthumously published journal, *A Vow of Conversation: Journals 1964-65*.

Dreams can be interpreted on two levels: the objective and the subjective. Objectively the dream is a commentary on the dreamer's external world; subjectively the dream is a commentary on the dreamer's inner world. In both cases, the message of the dream is best comprehended by symbolic interpretation. Jung maintained that dreams are the royal road to the unconscious. He writes:

> Dreams are often anticipatory and would lose their specific meaning on a purely causalistic view. They afford unmistakable information about the analytical situation, the correct understanding of which is of the greatest therapeutic importance.[2]

This is the appropriate time to address Merton's projection of his anima onto a woman. Michael Mott's biography corroborates Merton's romantic involvement with a nurse he met on March 31, 1966 when he was hospitalized for a back ailment.[3] Much has been made of this, but from a Jungian perspective this occurrence is understandable, if not to be expected. It is natural for a man to project his anima onto a woman; it is the psychological impetus for a man to fall in love with a woman, just as a woman falls in love with man as the result of her projection of her animus onto him.

The nurse, Mott calls S., is "dark Irish" and resembles in looks and age Merton's dream anima, Proverb.[4] Mott writes that Merton "was overwhelmed by the experience and it changed him forever."[5] Psychically it probably was the best thing that could have happened to Merton because, as Mott says, he never again referred to his inability to love, or to be loved, such was the gift of love and acceptance he received from S. and which he reciprocated.[6]

For Merton, as with all Cistercian monks, Mary the mother of God is theoretically the only acceptable recipient of anima projections. She is their patroness. Merton's full name is Father Louis Mary Merton. And every monk's last prayer at the end of the day at compline is the "Salve Regina." However, Mary's link with earth has been weakened because she has been raised so high into the rarified world of dogma with her "Immaculate Conception" and her "Assumption" of body and soul into heaven. Jung himself was jubilant when Pius XII declared in 1950 the dogma of the Assumption of the Blessed Virgin Mary. He writes:

> The new dogma affirms that Mary as the Bride is united with the Son in the heavenly bridal chamber, and as Sophia (Wisdom) she is united with the Godhead. Thus the feminine principle is brought into immediate proximity with the masculine Trinity.[7]

This recognition of the feminine in our culture was long overdue. But, Mary cannot be the recipient of instinctual longing or fantasy, a dilemma for all monks who take vows of celibacy.

Being aware of this psychological dynamic of projection, we can understand why so many men fail to take final vows as monks. And we can understand compassionately Merton's falling in love with his nurse who is mysteriously foreshadowed in his poem "Hagia Sophia." A monk's vocation is a special one; at the same time it is a rather difficult one. Monks need, however, contact with women who will assist them in getting in touch with the feminine within themselves. Permitting retreats for women at Gethsemani, as is now done, was a bold but wise decision.

In his journal *A Vow of Conversation* Merton records three dreams resonant of his continued, and positive confrontation with the feminine side of his personality. An examination of the third dream reveals that Merton has made progress in coming to terms with his first, negative experience of the feminine, that of his severe, demanding mother.

The anima figures of these three dreams appear under three distinctly different guises: a Lady Latinist, a Chinese princess, and a Black mother. It is enlightening to explore these dreams on both objective and subjective levels because they offer us important insights into Merton's outer and inner life.

It should be noted that because Merton recorded these dreams, he invites the reader to interpret them. Journals are composed of episodic and epigrammatic entries meant to be read slowly so that one can meditate on them in order to elicit their full import. And being a poet, Merton uses symbols; therefore, a symbolic reading of his dreams is one Merton himself would have been comfortable with. Jung himself says many times that the language of the soul is symbolic; he says, "Psychic development cannot be accomplished by intention and will alone; it needs the attraction of the symbol, whose value quantum exceeds that of cause."[8] It should be noted that Merton was quite familiar with Jungian theory. In a letter to Helen Wolf, Merton says, "I recently read Jung's *The Undiscovered Self* and want to say how much I enjoyed it and agreed with it. He is one of the rare men who are helping us rediscover the true shape of our life, and the true validity of our symbols."[9]

On March 10, 1964, Merton recorded the following dream:

> Last night I dreamed that a distinguished Lady Latinist came to give a talk to the novices on St. Bernard. Instead of a lecture, she sang in Latin meters, *flexes* and *puncta*. Something that sounded like the sermon of the saint, though I could not recognize it.

The novices were restive and giggled. This made me sad. In the middle of the performance the late abbot Dom Frederic, solemnly entered. We all stood. The singing was interrupted. I explained in an undertone that I had just now realized that the presence of this woman constituted a violation of cloister and I would remedy matters as soon as possible. Where did she come from, he asked. "Harvard," I said in a stage whisper which she must have heard. Then the novices were all on a big semi, loaded on the elevator, I don't know how, to go down from the top of the building. Instead of the Latinist coming on the elevator, I left the novices and escorted her down safely by the stairs: but now her clothes were all soiled and torn. She was confused and sad. She had no Latin and nothing much to say. I wonder what this dream is about. Is it about the Church? Is it about the liturgical revival, Anglicanism perhaps? Is it about some secret Anglican anima of my own?[10]

The Lady Latinist can be construed as the Catholic church. She represents the church before Vatican II; therefore, she is the rejected former church whose language is now considered archaic if not laughable, causing the novices to giggle. Merton is saddened by their reaction; he always loved the Latin language of the church; in fact, he never gave up reading his Latin breviaries which were with him even on his last trip to Asia.

The stairs symbolize the descent of this church, now soiled, worn, and in need of new clothes. The Lady is also confused and sad. The church of the sixties whose endeavors to modernize and update itself confused and saddened many Catholics. The Mass in the vernacular was the most controversial change for many; Merton himself, in favor of most of the liturgical changes, was saddened to see the Latin antiphons disappear forever. He continued to recite them privately.

Generally, Merton's dream reveals an ambiguity of response to the changing church of the sixties. The Lady Latinist represents the church Merton was received into on November 16, 1938 when he was baptized at Corpus Christi Church in New York. It was the Roman Catholic church he loved so much, the church that perhaps saved him from a life of dissipation. Although Merton does not defend the Lady Latinist, he does not abandon her. Concerned for her safety, he escorts her down the stairs, the archaic means of movement, while the novices take the modern means of descent, the elevator, symbolic of the ecumenical movement. Implied in Merton's choice of the stairs over the elevator is a criticism that perhaps the church is changing (moving) too quickly.

Dom Frederick Dunne is the male equivalent of the Lady Latinist. He represents the old order at Gethsemani, and had he lived (he died on August 4, 1948), he might have been disturbed by the changes of Vatican II. He was abbot of Gethsemani when Gregorian chant and the Latin Mass were the spiritual sustenance of Trappists monks. He was abbot before the basilica was stripped of its statues and altars. He was abbot when Merton entered Gethsemani; he encouraged Merton to continue to write his autobiography *The Seven Storey Mountain*; he handed to Merton the first copy of *The Seven Storey Mountain* on July 7, 1948.

His successor was Dom James Fox who led Gethsemani through the Vatican II period. He was also a graduate of Harvard's business school; he implemented sweeping changes at Gethsemani just as Vatican II would accomplish for the church. The old guard gives way to the new: the cycle of birth, death, and rebirth.

Subjectively this dream reveals that Merton is still not completely comfortable with the feminine aspects of his personality. The cloister is symbolic of the psyche; the problem is that there is no place for the feminine in a cloister which prohibits the presence of any woman. Furthermore, Merton himself does not comprehend her Latin singing. In other words anima and the dream-ego do not understand each other.

The novices and Dom Frederick are shadow figures in the dream: both question her presence. The novices mock it, reminding us of the mockers in Merton's Proverb dream. Merton's forgetting the cloister rule suggests an unconscious desire for the feminine, a desire not strong enough yet to withstand the presence of an authority figure like Dom Frederick who demands to know where she is from. All Merton can say is "Harvard."

Merton's dream-ego, therefore, does nothing to defend her presence in his cloister, his consciousness. He does not embrace her as he embraced Proverb, his anima figure of a previous dream, but escorts her from the cloister by descending the stairs, causing her to become more soiled and torn. All of this suggests that it is Merton who is torn or rather ambivalent about his anima (she is an aspect of his psyche), and by escorting her downstairs, symbolic of repression, he is avoiding his problem by returning his anima to the unconscious.

We could say that this is a negative dream offering little hope for psychic integration of the feminine (Merton seems to be regressing to his former unconscious state) except for the fact that the dream-ego is saddened by the novices and Dom Frederick's rejection, "This made me sad." The reader feels Merton's empathy and compassion for the Lady Latinist; so generally speaking we can view this as a positive dream regarding the anima.

In 1965, when writing in the journal later called *A Vow of Conversation*, Merton continued to refer to his "refusal of women." On July 7, 1965, he wrote to Sister Mary Luke Tobin recommending Karl Stern's new book, *The Flight from Woman,* saying "But you are not the ones who need it...."[11] Merton was conscious of his struggle to integrate the feminine into his life; consciousness of psychic imbalance facilitates its resolution.

On November 19, 1964, Merton recorded the following dream:

> Last night I had a haunting dream of a Chinese princess which stayed with me all day ("Proverb" again.) This lovely and familiar and archetypal person. (No "object" yet how close and real, and how elusive.) She comes to me in various mysterious ways in my dreams. This time she was with her "brothers," and I felt overwhelmingly the freshness, the youth, the wonder, the truth of her; her complete reality, more real than any other, yet unobtainable. Yet I deeply felt the sense of her understanding, knowing and loving me, in my depths—not merely in my individuality and everyday self, yet not as if this self were utterly irrelevant to her. (Not rejected, not accepted either.)[12]

The Chinese princess is an anima figure who represents Merton's interest in all things Eastern, including Chinese painting, Tao philosophy, and Zen Buddhism. The East is also the land of compassion, the land of nothingness, the tea ceremony, and calligraphy, all of which fascinated Merton.

As early as 1962, Merton began corresponding with Dr. John Wu who helped Merton learn Chinese, culminating in one of Merton's finest books, *The Way of Chuang Tzu* (Merton's favorite book) published in 1965 while the journal *A Vow of Conversation* was being written. The poetic interpretations of Chuang Tzu were very much on Merton's mind at the time of this dream. John Wu wrote to Merton on May 11, 1965 praising Merton's "nosegay of poems."[13] This made Merton ecstatic, writing in return: "What a wonderful letter that was! It was a pure delight, and it made me so happy that I had been insane enough to go ahead with the work on Chuang Tzu."[14] In June, 1963, over a year prior to the dream of the Chinese princess, Merton wrote of his new love, "Chuang Tzu is my delight."[15] It is no wonder that this so very positive dream reflects Merton's enriching study of Chuang Tzu which at one point he said "restores me to sanity."[16]

Because Merton's most numinous dreams of anima are those of Proverb, it is understandable that he would compare his Chinese princess to her. If we can credit Proverb with Merton's poem *Hagia Sophia*, perhaps we can credit his Chinese princess with his fine books on Zen: *Zen and the Birds of Appetite* and *Mystics and Zen Masters* and, of course, his poetic renditions of Chuang Tzu, *The Way of Chuang Tzu*.

As previously stated, the anima offers man the libido to develop further his personality (a woman's animus performs a similar function for her) which often results in a burst of creativity. Merton's Chinese princess makes available to him "freshness," "youth," "wonder," and "truth." How often men in late life fall in love with a younger woman and find themselves renewed, producing work of importance, if not genius. Artists like Yeats and Picasso are classic examples of such renewal inspired by a younger woman who becomes the artist's muse. Merton, a celibate, must rely on his inner woman.

This dream of anima invigorates Merton because he knows "in my depths," in his unconscious, that there is a figure who loves him for what he is and not just for his "everyday self," his ego and persona. He is loved for his complete self which also includes the negative, the shadow. There is a suggestion, however, that his anima and his ego are not completely in tune with each other, that there are some aspects of Merton's anima that are still "unobtainable," perhaps referring to Merton's belief that he was incapable of loving or accepting love. Merton's journal entry about this dream reveal that he has analyzed it carefully, seeking its meaning, trying to find what is "unobtainable." Jungian Marie Von France writes:

> But what does the role of the anima as guide to the inner world mean in practical terms? This positive function occurs when a man takes seriously the feelings, moods, expectations, and fantasies sent by his anima and when he fixes them in some form—for example, in writing, painting, sculpture, musical compositions, or dancing. When he works at this patiently and slowly, other more deeply unconscious material wells up from the depths and connects with the earlier material.[17]

On February 4, 1965, Merton recorded the following dream:

> Last night I had a curious and moving dream about a "black mother." I was in a place somewhere I had been as a child. I could not recognize it, but also there seemed to be some connection with Bell Hollow and I realized that I had come there for a reunion with a Negro foster mother whom I had loved in my childhood in the dream. Indeed it seemed, in the dream, that I owed my life to her, to her love for me, so that it was really she and not my natural mother who had given me life, as if from her had come a new life. And there she was. Her face was ugly and severe, yet a great warmth came from her to me and we embraced with love. I felt deep gratitude, and what I recognized was not her face but the warmth of her embrace and her heart, so to speak. Then we danced a little together, I and my black mother.
>
> Finally I had to continue the journey that I was on in my dream. I cannot remember any more about this journey or any incidents connected with it. The comings and goings, the turning back and so forth.[18]

Merton was very much concerned with racism in America and wrote eloquently about the Civil Rights Movement. His poems "And the Children of Birmingham" and "Picture of a Black Child with a White Doll" reveal his great compassion for the suffering of black children at the hands of white racists. One of his best friends, Merton's official biographer who died before completing his work, was John Howard Griffin, the author of the bestseller *Black Like Me*. A black anima figure certainly points to an empathy for and an identification with Black people in his conscious life; it also illustrates Merton's continuing all-embracing attitude toward the world.

In his autobiography Merton says little about his mother who died of cancer of the stomach when he was just six years old. She was a perfectionist whose demanding ways of rearing negatively affected her son. It is likely that this first experience of the feminine influenced Merton's "refusal of women." Marie Von France writes:

> In its individual manifestation the character of a man's anima is as a rule shaped by his mother. If he feels that his mother had a negative influence on him, his anima will often express itself in irritable, depressed moods, uncertainty, insecurity, and touchiness.[19]

Just a cursory glance at Merton's journals and letters reveal all of the above mentioned negative states of being which caused Merton a host of physical ailments from skin disease to insomnia, to stomach problems, to various forms of neuralgia.

He describes his mother in the first chapter of his autobiography (1948) as "thin and pale and rather severe." [20] The adjective "severe" appears again in his journal *The Sign of Jonas* (1953) when he says "perhaps solitaries are made by severe mothers."[21] And again in this dream he describes his black mother: "Her face was ugly and severe, yet a great warmth came from her to me and we embraced with love"—she is the antithesis of his natural mother.

An anima figure who is black and ugly is an anima figure that need not attract by being white or beautiful. Darkness is most often interpreted as evil, and beauty is held as the ideal of feminine perfection. But whiteness and beauty are not the essence of the feminine. In this dream, Merton, it seems, is not duped by appearance and accepts the gifts of the feminine which are love and warmth. He feels her love in the embrace, symbolic of the archetype *coniunctio*, suggesting the union of opposites and the birth of new possibilities. He then dances with her. The dance, too, is symbolic; its motion is circular; thus, it traces a mandala. Jung writes:

> The circle, as the symbol of completeness and perfect being, is a widespread expression for heaven, sun, and God; it is also the primordial image of man and the soul. [22]

The dream-ego's dance with his black mother enhances their union and harmony: subject and object have become one. Perhaps Merton has finally come to terms with his severe mother. Perhaps Merton, on a deep level, accepts the reality that although his mother *appeared* to be demanding and severe, she really loved him, that perhaps she herself, like her son, was uncomfortable in expressing love, but the love was always there. Thus, Merton feels a "deep gratitude."

The reference to Bell Hollow concerns a piece of land Gethsemani was considering purchasing for hermitages.[23] Merton lyrically describes the area; it is a pristine place where the water is pure. This is the land of his black mother. Such a positive dream can only mean that Merton was entering new territories of self-discovery and self-realization, a land of milk and honey.

A Lady Latinist, a Chinese princess, and a Black mother, three anima figures with important messages for Merton from his own unconscious. Any person who enters Jungian analysis will be instructed to record all remembered dreams, for they are truly hidden doors into the unconscious. Merton intuitively understood this truth. Furthermore, the title of this journal, *A Vow of Conversation*, suggests that even though Merton may be moving farther from people into his hermitage, he is completely committed to maintaining open dialogue with the world he loves; the title also suggests that Merton will remain conversant with his inner world, for Merton is also committed to open dialogue with the deepest aspects of his own psyche. As he says in one of his late poems:

> I went down
> Into the cavern
> All the way down
> To the bottom of the sea.
> I went down lower
> Than Jonas and the whale
> No one ever got so far down
> As me.[24]

Soon Merton's unpublished journals will be released to the public. It is likely that he recorded many more of his dreams; thus, Jungian analysis is a ripe exploratory tool for a deeper understanding of Merton's inner life, a tool that can also yield deeper insights not only into his dreams but also into his poetry, as done in the following chapter.

EIGHT

ALL THE WAY DOWN

I learn by going where I have to go.[1]

Merton's poem "All the Way Down" was written in 1966 when he was fifty-one years old. Found in the "uncollected poems" section of *The Collected Poetry of Thomas Merton*, "All the Way Down" can be interpreted as a retrospective view of Merton's individuation.

> I went down
> Into the cavern
> All the way down
> To the bottom of the sea.
> I went down lower
> Than Jonas and the whale
> No one ever got so far down
> As me.

Merton, the solitary explorer, admits his willingness to plumb the mystery of his psyche, to go "to the bottom of the sea." He proudly announces that he has penetrated the sea, symbol of the unconscious, more deeply than Jonas, the biblical figure Merton identified with as early as 1946 (*The Sign of Jonas*), twenty years before this poem was written.[2]

Merton, being a contemplative monk, is able to explore more deeply his psyche because the very nature of his vocation encourages him to do so. This exploration Merton considers an honor, one he wishes to share with others. He writes: "My brother, perhaps, in my solitude I have become as it were an explorer for you, a searcher in realms which you are not able to visit—except perhaps in the company of your psychiatrist."[3]

The poem itself is symbolic of Merton's willingness to reveal what he has discovered about himself to others because he knows that what is true for him is also true for all men and women, echoing Emerson's insight: "To believe your own thought, to believe that what is true for you in your private heart is true for all men—that is genius."[4]

> I went down lower
> Than any diamond mine
> Deeper than the lowest hole
> In Kimberly
> All the way down
> I thought I was the devil
> He was no deeper down
> Than me.

The first archetype to be encountered in the process of individuation is the shadow ("the devil"), an encounter which Jung says is the "apprentice-piece"[5] of a person's development; while coming to terms with one's contra-sexual archetype (animus/anima) is considered the "master-piece"[6] of individuation.

Often a person fails to integrate his shadow into consciousness because he is unwilling to face the negative aspects of his personality which he finds too disturbing; the truth about oneself is often painful. In order to preserve the idea he has of himself (his persona), he frequently projects his shadow onto other individuals, or onto a collective group or onto the world in general. Sometimes a person identifies with his shadow, believing he is completely evil. In this stanza Merton considers himself to be one of the world's greatest sinners, "I thought I was the devil."

As we have seen, Merton faced substantial obstacles with integrating his shadow into consciousness; as a Cistercian monk, however, he accomplished much shadow recognition/integration, eventually allowing him to take back his shadow projections which freed him to understand compassionately other people within his Trappist community and people in the outside world, resulting in a highly sensitive social consciousness that embraced all people.

The reference to diamond mines ("Kimberly") suggests that jewels are symbolic of the hidden treasures of self-knowledge that reside in "the lowest hole" of the psyche, gems of self-knowledge available to anyone willing to go "All the way down."

> And when they thought
> That I was gone forever
> That I was all the way
> In hell
> I got right back into my body
> And came back out
> And rang my bell.

The archetypal journey to wholeness requires the hero to pass through hell; the classic example of this is Dante's journey through *Inferno* and *Purgatorio*. Elements of Merton's consciousness ("And when they thought") feared he had gone down too far, but he returns to consciousness, represented by his body, and "rang my bell," a gesture suggesting a positive, if not joyful, encounter with the unconscious.

Bells are an important part of Merton's life. Gethsemani's tower bell announces all the liturgical hours of the day. The bells call all to prayer and holiness; they call all to God: "Bells are meant to remind us that God alone is good, that we belong to Him, that we are not living for this world. They tell us that we are His true temple. They call us to peace with Him within ourselves."[7] There is also the *Sanctus* bell announcing every day of a monk's life the presence of Christ at Mass.

Merton's first Mass at Gethsemani reverberated with the sound of bells:

> Almost simultaneously all around the church, at all the various altars, the bells began to ring. These monks, they rang no bells at the *Sanctus* or the *Hanc igitur*, only at the consecration: and now, suddenly, solemnly, all around the church, Christ was on the Cross, lifted up, drawing all things to Himself, that tremendous sacrifice tearing hearts from bodies, and them out to Him.[8]

Merton obeyed the clarion call that tears "hearts from bodies." He in effect obeyed the call to individuation. When Merton says he "rang my bell," he is truly summoning all people to embark on the inner journey, to find the Self, the Christ within, even though it requires their passing through hell ("I was all the way in hell"). Self-knowledge is costly, demanding suffering and purgation.

In his autobiography, Merton recounts the first Mass he ever attended, at Corpus Christ Church in New York City. He had not yet converted to Catholicism, but he obeyed his inner voice with its command to "Go to Mass! Go to Mass!"[9] Merton as a young man had visited the greatest churches and cathedrals of Europe, but he had never attended a Mass. And when he finally did, he was overjoyed. But at the sound of the bells at the consecration, he fled into the street because he felt he did not belong there for the "celebration of the Mysteries." He writes: "It was liturgically fitting that I should kick myself out at the end of the Mass of the Catechumens, when the ordained *ostiari* should have been there to do it."[10]

> No matter how
> They try to harm me now
> No matter where
> They lay me in the grave
> No matter what injustices they do
> I've seen the root
> Of all that believe.

What a person accomplishes in individuation cannot ever be taken away from him; no one can harm him because he is an integrated person. He is beyond harm because he is not ego-inflated; he knows who he is and where he came from, "I've seen the root/Of all that believe." He is whole. He has found the pearl of great price, or, if you will, the diamond "in the lowest hole." He, therefore, accepts the mote in another person's eye because he has seen and dealt with the beam in his own. He has befriended and accepted his shadow. Not even death, "No matter where/They lay me in the grave," can deprive him of the fruits of individuation, for he has been in touch with the "root of all that believe." He has experienced the collective unconscious from which springs all myth, all religion.

I've seen the room
Where life and death are made
And I have known
The secret forge of war
I even saw the womb
That all things come from
For I got down so far!

As all life originates in water, so all self-knowledge emerges from the deep waters of the psyche. Water is symbolic of the Great Mother, "the womb/That all things come from," the feminine principle, the universal womb, the *prima materia*. Merton compares the unconscious to a room under the sea, a secret room where life and death abide, where consciousness is born, where the old self dies so that the archetypal Self can be experienced, causing the ego to suffer a "sea change."

Again, self-knowledge demands arduous effort; it emerges from the struggle between ego and the Self. Forging, then, is an apt metaphor for individuation, "And I have known/The secret forge of War," suggesting the fires of a furnace with its power of transmutation. Water and fire: the marriage of opposites, leading to psychological wholeness.

But when they thought
I was gone forever
That I was all the way
In hell
I got right back into my body
And came back out
And rang my bell.

A deep sea diver knows he can descend so far into the ocean before he must return to the surface or risk drowning. When he returns to land, he then appreciates the wonders seen at the bottom of the sea, wonders he feels compelled to share with others. So too an individuated person must protect himself from being inundated by the waters of the unconscious; he must maintain a healthy ego-Self relationship. Jungian Edward Edinger writes:

> Individuation is a process, not a realized goal. Each new level of integration must submit to further transformation if development is to proceed. However, we do have some indications concerning what to expect as a result of the ego's conscious encounter with the Self. Speaking generally, the individuation urge promotes a state in which the ego is related to the Self without being identified with it.... The dichotomy between outer and inner reality is replaced by a sense of unitary reality.[11]

Because Merton has taken his individuation seriously, because he has made himself conscious of it, he has the privilege to ring his bell. The bell, containing qualities of the feminine and the masculine, is a symbol of completeness, of wholeness. Merton emerges from his encounter with the unconscious as a more complete/whole person; he is also energized with the libido (psychic energy) to ring his bell, to share with others the wonders of individuation.

Again we are reminded of the bells that called Merton from New York to his life as a Trappist at Gethsemani:

> I started to hear the great bell of Gethsemani ringing in the night—the bell in the big grey tower, ringing and ringing, as if it were just behind the first hill. The impression made me breathless, and I had to think twice to realize that it was only in my imagination that I was hearing the bell of the Trappist Abbey

ringing in the dark.... The bell seemed to be telling me where I belonged—as if it were calling me home.[12]

Merton listened to the bell. He writes: "My life is a listening. His is a speaking. My salvation is to hear and respond. For this, my life must be silent. Hence, my silence is my salvation."[13]

Merton, however, is not totally silent. His poetry and prose serve as a bell summoning all people to enter the waters of the psyche and embark on their own inner journey, one that calls every person "home," to the Christ within. Perhaps it is no coincidence that Merton was born on the last day of January, 1915, "under the sign of the Water Bearer."[14]

MERTON AND JUNG: CONTRASTS AND PARALLELS

The archetypal/universal nature of individuation is illustrated by the extraordinary similitude of insights that both Merton and Jung achieved along the way of their interior journey. This chapter will offer comparisons on a variety of important issues.

On Unity with the World

Merton: The contemplative is not isolated in himself, but liberated from his external and egotistic self by humility and purity of heart—therefore there is no longer any serious obstacle to simple and humble love of other men.[1]

Jung: Individuation does not shut one out from the world, but gathers the world to oneself.[2]

Creating Our Identity

Merton: Our vocation is not simply to be, but to work together with God in the creation of our own life, our own identity, our own destiny. We are free beings and sons of God. This means to say that we should not passively exist but actively participate in His creative freedom, in our own lives, and in the lives of others, by choosing truth.[3]

Jung: Every life is the realization of a whole, that is, of a self for which reason this can also be called "individuation." All life is bound to individual carriers who realize it, and it is simply inconceivable without them. But every carrier is charged with an individual destiny and destination, and the realization of these alone makes sense of life.[4]

Desire for God

Merton: To desire God is the most fundamental of all human desires. It is the very root of all our quest for happiness.[5]

Jung: "God" is a primordial experience of man, and from the remotest times humanity has taken inconceivable pains either to portray this baffling experience, to assimilate it by means of interpretation, speculation, and dogma, or else to deny it.[6]

The Heart

Merton: The concept of "the heart" might well be analyzed here. It refers to the deepest psychological ground of one's personality, the inner sanctuary where self-awareness goes beyond analytical reflection and opens one out into metaphysical and theological confrontation with the Abyss of the unknown and yet presents one who is "more intimate to us than we are to ourselves."[7]

Jung: The utterances of the heart—unlike those of the discriminating intellect—always relate to the whole. The heartstrings sing like an Aeolian harp only to the gentle breath of a premonitory mood, which does not drown the song but listens. What the heart hears are the great things that span our whole lives, the experience which we do nothing to arrange but which we ourselves suffer.[8]

God at the Center

Merton: One of the paradoxes of the mystical life is this: that a man cannot enter into the deepest center of himself and pass through that center into God, unless he is able to pass entirely out of himself and give himself to other people in the purity of love.[9]

Jung: It seems to me that it is only the person who seeks to realize his humanity who does God's will, not the one who takes flight before the sad fact "man." ... To become human seems to me to be the intention of God in us.[10]

The Mass

Merton: The divinizing and transforming action of God is exercised upon our souls in a very special way in the liturgy. The Mass is the privileged center of this divine action upon our inner freedom, because Christ is present, in the great redemptive fact of His death and resurrection, whenever bread and wine are validly consecrated in the Eucharistic sacrifice. Those who participate in the sacrifice enter into the mystery with Him.[11]

Jung: The Mass is the extramundane and extratemporal act in which Christ is sacrificed and then resurrected in the transformed substances; and this rite of his sacrificial death is not a repetition of the historical event but the original, unique and eternal act. The experience of the Mass is therefore a participation in the transcendence of life, which overcomes all bounds of space and time.[12]

The Hunger for Wholeness

Merton: There is something in the depths of our being that hungers for wholeness and finality. Because we are made for eternal life, we are made for an act that gathers up all powers and capacities of our being and offers them simultaneously and forever to God.[13]

Jung: The self is not only the center but also the whole circumference which embraces both conscious and unconscious; it is the center of this totality.[14]

Being Oneself

Merton: Every man has a vocation to be someone: but he must understand clearly that in order to fulfill this vocation he can only be one person: himself.[15]

Jung: One cannot live from anything except what one is.[16]

The Solitary Life

Merton: The solitary life, now that I really confront it, it is awesome, wonderful, and I see I have no strength of my own for it. Rather, I have a deep sense of my own poverty and, above all, an awareness of wrongs I have allowed myself together with this good desire ... the solitary life is not something that you can play at. Contrary to all that is said about it, I do not see how the really solitary life can tolerate illusion or self-deception.... It seems to me that solitude rips off all the masks and all the disguises. It tolerates no lies.[17]

Jung: The man whom we can with justice call "modern" is solitary. He is so of necessity and at all times, for every step towards a fuller consciousness of the present removes him further from his original "participation mystique" with the mass of men—from submersion in a common unconsciousness. Every step forward means an act of tearing himself loose from that all-embracing, pristine unconsciousness which claims the bulk of mankind almost entirely.... Indeed, he is completely modern only when he has come to the very edge of the world, leaving behind him all that has been discarded and outgrown, and acknowledging that he stands before a void out of which all things may grow.[18]

Exploring the Darkness

Merton: My brother, perhaps in my solitude I have become as it were an explorer for you, a searcher in realms which you are not able to visit—except perhaps in the company of your psychiatrist. I have been summoned to explore a desert area of man's heart in which explanations no longer suffice, and in which one learns that only experience counts, an arid, rocky, dark land of the soul, sometimes illuminated by strange fires which men fear and peopled by specters which men studiously avoid except in their nightmares.[19]

Jung: My entire youth can be understood in terms of this secret. It induced in me an almost unendurable loneliness. My one great achievement during those years was that I resisted the temptation to talk about it with anyone; thus, the pattern of my relationship to the world was already prefigured: today as then I am a solitary, because I know things and must hint at things which other people do not know, and usually do not even want to know.[20]

Chuang Tzu

To his friend Dr. John Wu, Merton wrote: I am so happy you are doing a study of Chuang Tzu, and I look forward to reading it, avidly. He is one of the great wise men: I will not say "philosophers" in the speculative sense, for his wisdom has a marvelous wholeness, and that is what makes it seem "simple." Indeed, it is simple, but at the same time utterly profound. I think he has in him an element which is essential to all true contemplation, and which is often lacking in Western "contemplatives."[21]

To his friend, Jung wrote: I have read your pamphlet with great interest and I can tell you that I fundamentally agree with your views. I see Taoism in the same light as you do. I'm a great admirer of Chuang Tzu's philosophy. I was again immersed in the study of his writings when your letter arrived in the midst of it. You are aware, of course, that Taoism formulates psychological principles which are of a very universal nature. As a matter of fact, they are so all-embracing that they are, as far as they go, applicable to any part of humanity.[22]

Locus Dei

Merton: Everything about this hermitage fills me with gladness. There are lots of things that could have been far more perfect one way or the other, ascetically or domestically, but it is the place God has given me after so much prayer and longing and without my deserving it, and it is a delight. I can imagine no other joy on earth than to have such a place to be at peace in. To live in silence, to think and write, to listen to the wind and to all the voices of the wood, to struggle with a new anguish, which is, nevertheless, blessed and secure, to live in the shadow of a big cedar cross, to prepare for my death and my exodus to the heavenly country, to love my brothers and all people, to pray for the whole world and offer peace and good sense among men. So it is my place in the scheme of things and that is sufficient. Amen.[23]

Jung: From the beginning I felt the Tower as in some way a place of maturation—a maternal womb or maternal figure in which I could become what I was, what I am and will be. At Bollingen I am in the midst of my true life, I am most deeply myself.... At times I feel as if I am spread out over the landscape and inside things, and I am myself living in every tree, in the splashing of the waves, in the clouds and animals that come and go, in the procession of the seasons. There is nothing in the Tower that has not grown into its own form over the decades, nothing with which I am not linked. Here everything has its history, and mine; here is space for the spaceless kingdom of the world and the psyche's hinterland.[24]

I Ching

Merton: You compare him (Pasternak) to Donne: I saw a very interesting analogy with an ancient Chinese book which Pasternak probably does not know at all. It is the *Book of Oracles* called the *I Ching*. This consists of a series of symbolic configurations of events or "changes" which one arrives at by drawing lots or tossing coins; but that is not the important thing. What is fascinating is the fact that each change is exactly that sort of fluid "style of movement" ... "arrangement of groups" ... which constitutes Pasternak's inclinations. Jung has written a fascinating preface to the *I Ching*, bringing in his archetypes.[25]

Jung: During the whole of those summer holidays I was preoccupied with the question: Are the *I Ching's* answers meaningful or not? If they are, how does the connection between psychic and physical sequence of events come about?[26]

God Alone

Merton: We crossed the court, climbed some steps, entered a high, dark hall. I hesitated on the brink of a polished, slippery floor, while the Brother groped for the light switch. Then, above another heavy door, I saw the words: "God alone."[27]

Jung: On his bookplate, on his gravestone, and on the doorway over his house in Kusnacht is this single inscription: "Vocatus atque non vocatus"—Summoned or not summoned, God will be present.[28]

GLOSSARY OF JUNGIAN TERMS

Active Imagination. It is a method of meditating imaginatively by which one may consciously enter into contact with the unconscious and make connection with psychic phenomena. More than anything, Active Imagination is a way of influencing the unconscious. It is a cyclic process: the unconscious produces a symbol; consciousness is inspired by it, reproduces it, forms it, and gives it expression; and this in turn influences the unconscious. Active Imagination gives symbolic expression to repressed contents, releasing them of their emotional energy.

Anima (Latin, "soul"). The unconscious, feminine aspect of a man's personality, his inner woman. She is personified in dreams by female figures ranging from harlot to witch to spiritual guide (Sophia). She is the Eros principle; therefore, a man's individuation is reflected in how he relates to people, especially women. Identification with a negative anima appears in a man as moodiness, obstinacy, and oversensitivity.

Animus (Latin, "spirit"). The unconscious, masculine aspect of a woman's personality. He personifies the Logos principle. Identification with the animus can cause a woman to be inflexible, opinionated, and disputatious. The animus is a woman's inner man who serves as a bridge between her ego and her own unconscious fecundity.

Archetype. Inherited universal patterns or motifs which abide in the collective unconscious. They serve as the basic foundation and structure of all religion and myth. They cannot be experienced directly, only indirectly through dreams and transcendental experiences.

Collective Unconscious. Whereas Freud is credited with the discovery of the personal unconscious (also called subconscious) mind, Jung is credited with the discovery of the collective unconscious (see his autobiography *Memories, Dreams, Reflections*). The collective unconscious is the abode of the archetypes.

Coniunctio (Latin, "uniting, joining together"). Jung sees this archetype as the marriage of opposites. A man coming to terms with his anima or a woman coming to terms with her animus experiences the psychic marriage of opposites which in turn results in rebirth and transformation.

Consciousness. A person's awareness, intuition, and perception, with a person's function of reflection as its achievement.

Contemptus Mundi (Latin, "contempt of the world"). To enter monastic life because one feels that the world is evil is to enter it for the wrong reason. One enters a monastery because one has a special contemplative vocation: to know, love, and serve God.

Dreams. Letters from the unconscious which reveal the hidden recesses of the psyche, and if reflected upon carefully, they can lead one to greater self-knowledge and wholeness.

Ego. The center of consciousness which in the first part of a person's life is dominant. A person's work in the second part of life is to foster the ego's realization of the Self.

Eros (Greek, "love"). The feminine principle of relatedness. In a man it is linked with his anima.

Ignis Fatuus (Latin, "foolish fire"). Will-o'-the-wisp; delusive hope. Jung considers a person's search for perfection as a delusion; in a lifetime a person can only hope to achieve wholeness.

Individuation. The process of the conscious realization of psychic reality. Its ultimate goal is the awareness of the Self.

Inflation. Too high or too low an opinion of one's self. Its antidote is self-knowledge.

Libido. Refers to energy. Freud sees libido as connected with sexuality. Jung sees libido in a more general fashion. In short, it is psychic energy, not just sexual energy. When a person is cured of neurosis, the individual experiences a flow of energy, libido.

Locus Dei (Latin, "place of God"). God is omnipresent, present not just in churches and monasteries. He is present in our souls.

Logos (Greek, "word"). The masculine principle of discrimination. In a woman it is linked with her animus.

Mandala. From the Sanscrit word meaning "magic circle." It can be a geometric figure of a squared or circled square. It is a symbol of the Self; therefore, it is a symbol of wholeness.

Numinous. Jung sees numinosity in an event that possesses a quality of the spiritual or the transcendent as if it happened by/with God's consent. Thus numinous events are not only holy but also fateful.

Persona (Latin, "actor's mask"). The face we present to the world. The danger is that over-identification with the persona hinders self-knowledge since the persona represents only our social role.

Projection. The process by which an unconscious quality or trait is cast onto others (including collective things like races and countries and cities). Projection of the anima or animus onto a real woman or man is the dynamic of falling in love. The danger is that we make people in our own image, instead of seeing them as they really are.

Self. The archetype of wholeness which is also the regulating center of the personality. For Western man the Self is Christ.

Shadow. Unconscious characteristics or traits of the personality which the ego tends to reject, deny or ignore. It is personified in dreams by figures of the same sex as the dreamer. Consciously integrating the shadow into our life is one of the main tasks of individuation, a task which leads to an increase of energy.

Synchronicity. A causal connecting principle. Jung describes synchronicity as a "meaningful coincidence" between the outer world and the inner world.

Unconscious. Jung sees the unconscious as that portion of the psyche that is not available to the conscious mind. It is everything which is not known or available to the ego, the center of consciousness.

NOTES

PREFACE

1. Anne E. Carr, *A Search for Wisdom and Spirit: Thomas Merton's Theology of the Self* (Notre Dame, IN: University of Notre Dame Press, 1988), p. 128.

INTRODUCTION

1. Ralph Waldo Emerson, "Self-Reliance," *Basic Selections from Emerson*, ed. by Eduard C. Lindeman (New York: Mentor Book, 1954), p. 53.

2. Carl Jung, *Memories, Dreams, Reflections* (New York: Random House, 1961), xi.

3. Carl Jung, *Modern Man in Search of a Soul* (New York: Harvest, 1933), p. 229.

4. "C. G. Jung A Mystic?" Interview with Aniela Jaffe, *Psychological Perspectives* (Spring-Summer, 1988), pp. 86-87.

5. Miguel Serrano, *C. G. Jung and Hermann Hesse: A Record of Two Friendships* (New York: Schocken Books, 1965), p. 56.

6. Andrew Samuels, Bani Shorter, and Fred Plaut, *A Critical Dictionary of Jungian Analysis* (New York: Routledge and Kegan Paul, 1986), p. 76. Thomas Merton, *New Seeds of Contemplation* (New York: New Directions Books, 1962), p. 64.

7. Carl Jung, *Selected Letters of C. G. Jung, 1909-1961*, ed. by Gerhard Adler and Aniela Jaffe (Princeton: Princeton University Press, 1953), p. 140.

8. Carl Jung, *Psychological Reflections: A New Anthology of His Writings*, ed. by Jolande Jacobi (New York: Bollingen Foundations Inc., 1973), p. 219.

9. Thomas Merton, *The School of Charity*, letters ed. by Patrick Hart (New York: Farrar, Straus, and Giroux, 1990), p. 384.

10. Thomas Merton, *Life and Holiness* (New York: Herder and Herder, 1963), pp. 15-16.

11. Daryl Sharp, *C. G. Jung Lexicon: A Primer of Terms and Concepts* (Toronto: Inner City Books, 1991), p. 22.

12. Sharp, p. 22.

13. Thomas Merton, *The Sign of Jonas* (New York: Harcourt, Brace and Company, 1953), pp. 18-19.

ONE

1. Samuels, p. 138.

2. Samuels, p. 138.

3. Carl Jung, *Psyche and Symbol* (Garden City, NY: Anchor Books, 1958), p. 8.

4. William Shakespeare, *The Tempest*, Act V, Sc. I.

5. Jolande Jacobi, *The Way of Individuation* (New York: Harcourt, Brace and Co., 1965), p. 25.

6. Thomas Merton, *The Seven Storey Mountain* (New York: Harcourt, Brace and Co., 1948), p. 82.

7. Dante Alighieri, *The Divine Comedy*, trans. by Mandelbaum (New York: Bantam Books, 1986), p. 3.

8. Merton, *Mountain*, p. 85.

9. Merton, *Mountain*, p. 85.

10. Merton, *Mountain*, p. 99.

11. Merton, *Mountain*, p. 10.

12. Monica Furlong, *Merton, A Biography* (New York: Harper and Row, 1980), p. 60.

13. Michael Mott, *The Seven Mountains of Thomas Merton* (Boston: Houghton Mifflin, 1985), p. 25.

14. Simone Weil, *The Simone Weil Reader: A Legendary Spiritual Odyssey of Our Time* (New York: David McKay Co. Inc, 1977), p. 379.

15. Thomas Merton, *No Man Is an Island* (New York: Harcourt Brace Jovanovich, 1983), p. 34.

16. Merton, *Mountain*, p. 111.

17. Merton, *Mountain*, p. 111.

18. Esther Harding, *Journey to the Self* (New York: Longmans, Green and Co., Inc., 1956), p. 27.

19. Jung, *Psychological Reflections*, p. 315.

TWO

1. Jung, *Psychological Reflections*, p. 224.

2. Merton, *Mountain*, p. 118.

3. Merton, *Mountain*, p. 68.

4. Merton, *Mountain*, p. 123.

5. Merton, *Mountain*, p. 126.

6. Carl Jung, *Collected Works of C. G. Jung*, 20 Vols., trans. by R. F. C. Hull (Princeton, NJ: Princeton University Press, 1953-1979), Vol. 16, p. 389.

7. Merton, *Mountain*, p. 113.

8. Merton, *Mountain*, p. 121.

9. Merton, *Mountain*, p. 121.

10. Mott, p. 80.

11. Furlong, p. 58.

12. Furlong, p. 60.

13. Merton, *Mountain*, p. 126.

14. Jung, *Psychological Reflections*, p. 315.

15. Mott, p. 78.

16. Merton, *Mountain*, p. 133.

17. Theodore Roethke, *The Collected Poems of Theodore Roethke* (New York: Anchor Press, 1975), p. 156.

THREE

1. Roethke, p. 231.

2. Mott, p. 90.

3. Merton, *Mountain*, p. 137.

4. Roethke, p. 231.

5. Jung, *Collected Works*, Vol. 9, Part 1, p. 123.

6. Merton, *Mountain*, p. 162.

7. Calvin Hall and Vernon J. Nordy, *A Primer of Jungian Psychology* (New York: Taplinger Publishing Co. 1973), p. 47.

8. Thomas Merton, *A Vow of Conversation: Journals 1964-65* (New York: Farrar, Straus, and Giroux, 1988), p. 132.

9. Anthony Stevens, *On Jung* (London: Penguin, 1990), p. 102.

10. Samuels, p. 87.

11. Merton, *Mountain*, p. 189.

12. Merton, *Mountain*, p. 204.

13. C. G. Jung, *Visions Seminars, Vol. 2* (Zurich: Spring Publications, 1976), pp. 409-410.

14. Jung, *Psychological Reflections*, p. 364.

15. Samuels, p. 100.

16. Samuels, p. 100.

17. Merton, *Mountain*, p. 284.

18. Merton, *Mountain*, p. 285.

19. Dante, p. 301.

FOUR

1. Merton, *New Seeds*, p. 60.

2. Merton, *Mountain*, p. 409.

3. William Shannon, *Silent Lamp* (New York: Crossroad, 1992), p. 130.

4. Thomas Merton, *Seeds of Contemplation* (New York: New Directions, 1949), p. 60.

5. Merton, *Seeds*, p. 70 (italics added).

6. Merton, *Seeds*, p. 124.

7. Merton, *Seeds*, p. 28 (italics added).

8. Thomas Merton, *The Waters of Siloe* (New York: Harcourt and Brace, 1949), p. 349.

9. Sharp, p. 49.

10. Merton, *Seeds*, p. 22.

11. Merton, *Seeds*, p. 35 (italics added).

12. Merton, *Seeds*, p. 41.

13. Merton, *The Sign of Jonas*, p. 91.

14. Jacobi, *The Way of Individuation*, p. 41.

15. Jung, *Psychological Reflections*, p. 253.

16. William Shakespeare, *King Lear*, Act III, Sc. IV.

FIVE

1. Thomas Merton, *The Road to Joy, Letters to New and Old Friends*, ed. by Robert Daggy (New York: Farrar, Straus, and Giroux, 1989), p. 208.

2. David D. Cooper, *Thomas Merton's Art of Denial: The Evolution of a Radical Humanist* (Athens: University of Georgia Press, 1989), p. 37.

3. Jolande Jacobi, *Complex, Archetype, Symbol in the Psychology of C. G. Jung* (New York: Princeton University Press, 1959), p. 155.

4. Jung, *Psychological Reflections*, p. 228.

5. Jung, *Psychological Reflections*, p. 28.

6. C. G. Jung, *Memories, Dreams, Reflections* (New York: Random House, 1961), p. 196.

7. Samuels, p. 138.

8. Thomas Merton, *Faith and Violence: Christian Teaching and Christian Practice* (Notre Dame, IN: University Notre Dame Press, 1968), p. 213.

9. Merton, *The Sign of Jonas*, p. 354.

10. Jung, *Psychological Reflections*, p. 316.

11. Jung, *Psychological Reflections*, p. 316.

12. Jung, *Memories*, p. 161.

13. Jung, *Psychological Reflections*, p. 53.

SIX

1. Sharp, p. 19.

2. John Sanford, *Invisible Partners* (New York: Paulist Press, 1980), pp. 65-66.

3. Jung, *Memories*, p. 186.

4. Jung, *Memories*, p. 187.

5. Mott, p. 312.

6. Merton, *A Vow*, pp. 193-194.

7. Merton, *Mountain*, p. 115.

8. Mott, p. 313.

9. Jung, source unknown.

10. Merton, *The Sign of Jonas*, p. 262.

11. Sharp, p. 22.

12. Mott, p. 311.

13. Mott, p. 311.

14. Cooper, p. 143.

15. Thomas Merton, *Contemplation in a World of Action* (London: Unwin, 1971), p. 149.

16. Mott, p. 313.

17. Mott, p. 313.

18. Mott, p. 313.

19. Mott, p. 313.

20. Mott, p. 317.

21. Mott, p. 326.

22. Mott, p. 326.

23. Thomas Merton, *The Collected Poems of Thomas Merton* (New York: New Directions Books, 1977), p. 363.

24. Mott, p. 362.

SEVEN

1. Jung, *Psychological Reflections*, p. 53.

2. Jung, *Psychological Reflections*, p. 60.

3. Mott, p. 437.

4. Mott, p. 435.

5. Mott, p. 438.

6. Mott, p. 438.

7. Jung, *Memories*, p. 202.

8. Jung, *The Collected Works*, Vol. 8, p. 47.

9. Thomas Merton, *The Courage for Truth: Letters to Writers*, ed. by Christine M. Bochen (New York: Farrar, Straus, and Giroux, 1993), pp. 97-98.

10. Merton, *A Vow*, pp. 32-33.

11. Merton, *The School of Charity*, p. 287.

12. Merton, *A Vow*, p. 101.

13. Thomas Merton, *The Hidden Ground of Love, Letters*, ed. by William Shannon (New York: Farrar, Straus, and Giroux, 1985), p. 627.

14. Merton, *Hidden Ground*, p. 627.

15. Merton, *Hidden Ground*, p. 624.

16. Merton, *Hidden Ground*, p. 623.

17. M. L. von France, "The Process of Individuation," in *Man and His Symbols*, ed. by Carl Jung (New York: Dell Publishing Co., 1964), p. 195.

18. Merton, *A Vow*, p. 144.

19. von France, p. 186.

20. Merton, *Mountain*, p. 15.

21. Merton, *The Sign of Jonas*, p. 262.

22. Sharp, p. 110.

23. Merton, *A Vow*, p. 130.

24. Merton, *The Collected Poems*, p. 669.

EIGHT

1. Roethke, p. 104.

2. Merton, *The Sign of Jonas*, p. 17.

3. Thomas Merton, "A Letter on the Contemplative Life," in *The Monastic Journey*, ed. by Brother Patrick Hart, pp. 220-221.

4. Emerson, "Self-Reliance," p. 53.

5. Sharp, p. 22.

6. Sharp, p. 22.

7. Thomas Merton, *Thoughts in Solitude* (New York: Noonday Press, Farrar, Straus, and Giroux, 1956), p. 67.

8. Merton, *Mountain*, pp. 323-324.

9. Merton, *Mountain*, p. 206.

10. Merton, *Mountain*, p. 210.

11. Edward F. Edinger, *Ego and Archetype* (New York: Penguin, 1972), p. 96.

12. Merton, *Mountain*, pp. 364-365.

13. Merton, *Thoughts*, p. 72.

14. Merton, *Mountain*, p. 3.

NINE

1. Merton, *New Seeds*, p. 66.

2. Jung, *Psychological Reflections*, p. 317.

3. Merton, *New Seeds*, p. 32.

4. Jung, *Psychological Reflections*, p. 316.

5. Merton, *New Seeds*, p. 5.

6. Jung, *Psychological Reflections*, p. 316.

7. Thomas Merton, *The Climate of Monastic Prayer* (Spencer, MA: Cistercian Publications, 1969), p. 38.

8. Jung, *Psychological Reflections*, p. 259.

9. Merton, *New Seeds*, p. 64.

10. Carl Jung, *C. G. Jung: Letters* (Princeton, NJ: Princeton University Press, 1975), pp. 28-29.

11. Thomas Merton, *The New Man* (New York: Farrar, Straus, and Cudahy, 1961), p. 233.

12. Jung, *Psychological Reflections*, p. 364.

13. Merton, *No Man*, p. 140.

14. Jung, *Memories*, p. 398.

15. Merton, *No Man*, p. 133.

16. Jung, *Psychological Reflections*, p. 311.

17. Merton, *A Vow*, p. 204.

18. Carl Jung, *Modern Man in Search of a Soul* (New York: Harcourt, Brace and World, 1933), p. 197.

19. Merton, "A Letter on the Contemplative Life," pp. 220-21.

20. Jung, *Memories*, pp. 41-42.

21. Merton, *Hidden Ground*, p. 613.

22. Jung, *Selected Letters*, pp. 97-98.

23. Merton, *A Vow*, p. 152.

24. Jung, *Memories*, p. 225.

25. Merton, *Hidden Ground*, p. 389.

26. Jung, *Memories*, p. 225.

27. Merton, *Mountain*, p. 358.

28. Wayne G. Rollins, *Jung and the Bible* (Atlanta: John Knox Press, 1983), p. 127.

BIBLIOGRAPHY

Alighieri, Dante. *The Divine Comedy*, trans. by Allen Mandelbaum. New York: Bantam Books, 1988.

Cooper, David D. *Thomas Merton's Art of Denial: The Evolution of a Radical Humanist*. Athens: University of Georgia Press, 1989.

Edinger, Edward F. *Ego and Archetype*. New York: Penguin, 1972.

Emerson, Ralph Waldo. *Basic Selections from Emerson*, ed. by Eduard C. Lindeman. New York: Mentor Books, 1954.

Furlong, Monica. *Merton, A Biography*. New York: Harper and Row, 1980.

Harding, Esther. *Journey to the Self*. New York: Longmans, Green and Co., Inc., 1956.

Jacobi, Jolande. *Complex, Archetype, Symbol in the Psychology of C. G. Jung*. Princeton, NJ: Princeton University Press, 1959.

_____ . *The Way of Individuation*. New York: Harcourt, Brace and Company, 1965.

Jung, Carl. *C. G. Jung: Letters*, ed. by Gerhard Adler. Princeton, NJ: Princeton University Press, 1975.

_____ . *Man and His Symbols*. New York: Dell Publishing Co. 1964.

_____ . *Memories, Dreams, Reflections*. New York: Random House, 1961.

_____ . *Modern Man in Search of a Soul*. New York: Harcourt, Brace and World, 1933.

_____ . *Psychological Reflections: A New Anthology of His Writings*, ed. by Jolande Jacobi and R. F. C. Hull. New York: Bollingen Foundation, 1970.

_____ . *Selected Letters of C. G. Jung, 1909-1961*, ed. by Gerhard Adler and Aniela Jaffe. Princeton, NJ: Princeton University Press, 1984.

_____ . *The Collected Works of C. G. Jung*, 20 Vols., trans. by R. F. C. Hull. Princeton, NJ: Princeton University Press, 1953-1979.

Malits, Elena. *The Solitary Explorer, Thomas Merton's Transforming Journey*. New York: Harper and Row Publishers, 1980.

Mott, Michael. *The Seven Mountains of Thomas Merton*. Boston: Houghton Mifflin, 1984.

Roethke, Theodore. *The Collected Poems of Theodore Roethke*. New York: Anchor Press, 1975.

Rollins, Wayne G. *Jung and the Bible*. Atlanta: John Knox Press, 1983.

Samuels, Andrew, Bani Shorter and Fred Plaut. *A Critical Dictionary of Jungian Analysis*. New York: Routledge and Kegan Paul, 1986.

Sanford, John. *Invisible Partners*. New York: Paulist Press, 1980.

Serrano, Miguel. *C. G. Jung and Hermann Hesse: A Record of Two Friendships*. New York: Schocken Books, 1965.

Sharp, Daryl. *C. G. Jung Lexicon: A Primer of Terms and Concepts*. Toronto: Inner City Books, 1991.

Stevens, Anthony. *On Jung*. London: Penguin, 1990.

Weil, Simone. *The Simone Weil Reader: A Legendary Spiritual Odyssey of Our Time*. New York: David McKay Co. Inc., 1977.

SELECTED BIBLIOGRAPHY OF BOOKS
BY THOMAS MERTON

The Ascent to Truth. New York: Harcourt, Brace, 1951.

The Asian Journal of Thomas Merton, ed. by Naomi Burton, Brother Patrick Hart, and James Laughlin. New York: New Directions, 1973.

Bread in the Wilderness. New York: New Directions, 1952.

The Climate of Monastic Prayer. Spencer, MA: Cistercian Publications, 1969.

The Collected Poems of Thomas Merton. New York: New Directions Books, 1977.

Conjectures of a Guilty Bystander. New York: Doubleday, 1966.

Contemplative Prayer. New York: Doubleday, 1966.

Contemplation in a World of Action. New York: Doubleday, 1966.

The Courage for Truth: Letters to Writers, ed. by Christine M. Bochen. New York: Farrar, Straus, and Giroux, 1993.

Disputed Questions. New York: Farrar, Straus, and Cudahy, 1960.

Faith and Violence: Christian Teaching and Christian Practice. Notre Dame, IN: University of Notre Dame Press, 1968.

The Hidden Ground of Love (letters), ed. by William Shannon. New York: Farrar, Straus, and Giroux, 1985.

Life and Holiness. New York: Doubleday, 1964.

The Living Bread. New York: Farrar, Straus and Cudahy, 1956.

The Monastic Journey, ed. by Brother Patrick Hart. New York: Doubleday, 1978.

My Argument with the Gestapo: A Macaronic Journal. New York: Doubleday, 1969.

Mystics and Zen Masters. New York: Farrar, Straus, and Giroux, 1967.

The New Man. New York: Farrar, Straus, and Cudahy, 1961.

New Seeds of Contemplation. New York: New Directions, 1961.

No Man Is an Island. New York: Harcourt, Brace, 1955.

The Non-Violent Alternative, ed. by Gordon C. Zahn. New York: Farrar, Straus, and Giroux, 1980.

Praying the Psalms. Collegeville, MN: Liturgical Press, 1956.

Raids on the Unspeakable. New York: New Directions, 1966.

The Road to Joy: Letters to New and Old Friends, ed. by Robert Daggy. New York: Farrar, Straus, and Giroux, 1989.

The School of Charity: Letters, ed. by Patrick Hart. New York: Farrar, Straus, and Giroux, 1990.

The Secular Journal of Thomas Merton. New York: Doubleday, 1969.

Seeds of Contemplation. New York: New Directions, 1949.

The Seven Storey Mountain. New York: Harcourt, Brace, 1948.

The Sign of Jonas. New York: Harcourt, Brace, 1953.

The Silent Life. New York: Farrar, Straus, and Cudahy, 1957.

Spiritual Direction and Meditation. Collegeville, MN: Liturgical Press, 1960.

Thoughts in Solitude. New York: Doubleday, 1968.

Thomas Merton on Peace, ed. by Gordon C. Zahn. New York: McCall, 1971.

Thomas Merton in Alaska: The Alaskan Conferences, Journals, and Letters, ed. by Robert E. Daggy. New York: A New Directions Book, 1988.

A Thomas Merton Reader, ed. by Thomas P. McDonnell. New York: Doubleday, 1962.

A Vow of Conversation: Journals 1964-65. New York: Farrar, Straus, and Giroux, 1988.

The Waters of Siloe. New York: Harcourt, Brace, 1949.

The Way of Chuang Tzu. New York: New Directions, 1965.

What Is Contemplation? London: Burns, Oates and Washbourne, 1950.

The Wisdom of the Desert. New York: New Directions, 1960.

Zen and the Birds of Appetite. New York: New Directions, 1968.